W9-AFT-055

National Security

Other Books of Related Interest:

Opposing Viewpoints Series

America's Global Influence

Iran

North & South Korea

Rogue Nations

At Issue Series

Can Democracy Succeed in the Middle East?

Can the War on Terrorism Be Won?

Is Iran a Threat to Global Security?

What Are the Most Serious Threats to National Security?

Current Controversies Series

America's Battle Against Terrorism

Developing Nations

Weapons of Mass Destruction

"Congress shall make no law . . . abridging the freedom of speech, or of the press."

First Amendment to the U.S. Constitution

The basic foundation of our democracy is the First Amendment guarantee of freedom of expression. The Opposing Viewpoints series is dedicated to the concept of this basic freedom and the idea that it is more important to practice it than to enshrine it.

OPPOSING VIEWPOINTS® SERIES

National Security

David Haugen, Book Editor

GREENHAVEN PRESS

An imprint of Thomson Gale, a part of The Thomson Corporation

THOMSON
™
GALE

Detroit • New York • San Francisco • New Haven, Conn. • Waterville, Maine • London

NOV 1 5 2007

THOMSON
GALE
™

Christine Nasso, *Publisher*
Elizabeth Des Chenes, *Managing Editor*

© 2007 The Gale Group.

Star logo is a trademark and Gale and Greenhaven Press are registered trademarks used herein under license.

For more information, contact:
Greenhaven Press
27500 Drake Rd.
Farmington Hills, MI 48331-3535
Or you can visit our Internet site at http://www.gale.com

Articles in Greenhaven Press anthologies are often edited for length to meet page require- ments. In addition, original titles of these works are changed to clearly present the main thesis and to explicitly indicate the author's opinion. Every effort is made to ensure that Greenhaven Press accurately reflects the original intent of the authors. Every effort has been made to trace the owners of copyrighted material.

Cover photograph reproduced by permission of photos.com.

LIBRARY OF CONGRESS CATALOGING-IN-PUBLICATION DATA

National security / David Haugen, book editor
   p. cm. -- (Opposing viewpoints)
   Includes bibliographical references and index.
   ISBN-13: 978-0-7377-3761-5 (hardcover)
   ISBN-13: 978-0-7377-3762-2 (pbk.)
   1. National security--United States--Juvenile literature. 2. Terrorism--United
States--Prevention--Juvenile literature. 3. Threats of violence--Juvenile literature.
4. World politics--21st century--Juvenile literature. I. Haugen, David M., 1969-
   UA927.N38 2007
   355'.033073--dc22

                        2007024926

ISBN-10: 0-7377-3761-1 (hardcover)
ISBN-10: 0-7377-3762-X (pbk.)

Printed in the United States of America
10 9 8 7 6 5 4 3 2 1

Contents

Chapter 3: Are U.S. Homeland Security Measures Effectively Countering Terrorism?

Why Consider Opposing Viewpoints?

> "The only way in which a human being can make some approach to knowing the whole of a subject is by hearing what can be said about it by persons of every variety of opinion and studying all modes in which it can be looked at by every character of mind. No wise man ever acquired his wisdom in any mode but this."
>
> John Stuart Mill

In our media-intensive culture it is not difficult to find differing opinions. Thousands of newspapers and magazines and dozens of radio and television talk shows resound with differing points of view. The difficulty lies in deciding which opinion to agree with and which "experts" seem the most credible. The more inundated we become with differing opinions and claims, the more essential it is to hone critical reading and thinking skills to evaluate these ideas. Opposing Viewpoints books address this problem directly by presenting stimulating debates that can be used to enhance and teach these skills. The varied opinions contained in each book examine many different aspects of a single issue. While examining these conveniently edited opposing views, readers can develop critical thinking skills such as the ability to compare and contrast authors' credibility, facts, argumentation styles, use of persuasive techniques, and other stylistic tools. In short, the Opposing Viewpoints series is an ideal way to attain the higher-level thinking and reading skills so essential in a culture of diverse and contradictory opinions.

In addition to providing a tool for critical thinking, Opposing Viewpoints books challenge readers to question their own strongly held opinions and assumptions. Most people form their opinions on the basis of upbringing, peer pressure, and personal, cultural, or professional bias. By reading carefully balanced opposing views, readers must directly confront new ideas as well as the opinions of those with whom they disagree. This is not to simplistically argue that everyone who reads opposing views will—or should—change his or her opinion. Instead, the series enhances readers' understanding of their own views by encouraging confrontation with opposing ideas. Careful examination of others' views can lead to the readers' understanding of the logical inconsistencies in their own opinions, perspective on why they hold an opinion, and the consideration of the possibility that their opinion requires further evaluation.

Evaluating Other Opinions

To ensure that this type of examination occurs, Opposing Viewpoints books present all types of opinions. Prominent spokespeople on different sides of each issue as well as well-known professionals from many disciplines challenge the reader. An additional goal of the series is to provide a forum for other, less-known, or even unpopular viewpoints. The opinion of an ordinary person who has had to make the decision to cut off life support from a terminally ill relative, for example, may be just as valuable and provide just as much insight as a medical ethicist's professional opinion. The editors have two additional purposes in including these less-known views. One, the editors encourage readers to respect others' opinions—even when not enhanced by professional credibility. It is only by reading or listening to and objectively evaluating others' ideas that one can determine whether they are worthy of consideration. Two, the inclusion of such viewpoints encourages the important critical thinking skill of objectively evaluating an author's credentials and bias. This evaluation will illuminate an author's reasons for taking a particular stance on an issue and will aid in readers' evaluation of the author's ideas.

It is our hope that these books will give readers a deeper understanding of the issues debated and an appreciation of the complexity of even seemingly simple issues when good and honest people disagree. This awareness is particularly important in a democratic society such as ours in which people enter into public debate to determine the common good. Those with whom one disagrees should not be regarded as enemies but rather as people whose views deserve careful examination and may shed light on one's own.

Thomas Jefferson once said that "difference of opinion leads to inquiry, and inquiry to truth." Jefferson, a broadly educated man, argued that "if a nation expects to be ignorant and free . . . it expects what never was and never will be." As individuals and as a nation, it is imperative that we consider the opinions of others and examine them with skill and discernment. The Opposing Viewpoints series is intended to help readers achieve this goal.

David L. Bender and Bruno Leone,
Founders

Introduction

*"The potential for surprise, the blurring
of war and peace, the lack of a distinct
battlefield, and the sheer number of possible adversaries that threaten American
interests at home and abroad is unprecedented in our history as a nation."*

—*Peter Brookes,*
The Devil's Triangle:
Terrorism, Weapons of Mass
Destruction, and Rogue States

Media pundits and political analysts assert that the initial
years of the twenty-first century have borne witness to
the Age of Terrorism. The stunning and brazen attack on the
American homeland on September 11, 2001, ushered in this
new age and exemplified to the nation and to the world that
global security was anything but assured. In previous decades,
the United States and the rest of the free world had faced off
against the Soviet Union and its Communist allies, but the resulting Cold War remained cold in part because huge conventional armies and a mutual threat of nuclear devastation en-
sured that national security on either side was protected short
of a declaration of war. Since September 11, the security and
retaliatory powers of the United States and other convention-
ally powerful nations seems in doubt. Besides the crashing of
jetliners into American landmarks, small groups of operatives
have detonated bombs in Egypt, England, India, and Spain,
and nearly succeeding to do so in Germany as well. All of
these acts have come without warning, and their perpetrators
have eschewed military targets to strike at vulnerable civilian
populations. Such unorthodox warfare has caught many countries off guard and proved that national security may be a
relative term.

For the United States, the definition of national security has changed in light of the September 11 attacks. During the Cold War, Asian nations such as Korea and Vietnam bore the brunt of military confrontation between democracy and communism, and Europe was the anticipated site of any altercation between East and West. Protected by two oceans, the United States would be an unlikely and impractical target of Soviet invasion. In the Age of Terrorism, however, American cities are on the front lines, and all points on the globe appear equally susceptible to terrorist acts. In addition, though terrorism had existed before September 11, its character has changed in the new era. As Brigadier General Russ Howard claims, "The new terrorism is more violent. Under the old paradigm, terrorists wanted attention, not mass casualties. Now they want both." To thwart such devastation, national security enforcers have placed their faith in increased surveillance, homeland defense agencies, and taking the fight—both militarily and politically—overseas to the nations that breed and harbor terrorists. The United States waged war in Afghanistan and later in Iraq, in part, to root out terrorist training grounds and topple regimes supposedly sympathetic to terrorists' anti-American cause.

Beyond the concern for its namesakes, the Age of Terrorism has also been marked by the proliferation of weapons of mass destruction and the destabilizing powers of rogue states—the two other legs of what Heritage Foundation fellow Peter Brookes calls "the Devil's Triangle." Both of these concerns have lately become embodied by North Korea and Iran, two nations that have governments that are openly antagonistic toward America and have active programs to build nuclear weapons. Such countries have become a priority of U.S. national security advisers because these nations not only have the influence to destabilize regions (especially if they become nuclear), but also because their unfriendly regimes may, in the words of President George W. Bush, "give or sell those weapons to terrorist allies, who would use them without the least hesitation." Brookes suggests that each side of his Devil's Triangle is enough to worry defense agencies, but "a relationship between the three presents the United States and the international community with their greatest national security challenge in years."

Many commentators, such as Stephen Flynn, a member of the Council on Foreign Relations, believe that America is not prepared to face the threats that beset it in this new age. Recognizing that the nation is no longer geographically sheltered, Flynn bemoans the fact that the United States has not taken the proper precautions to strengthen its defense and address its vulnerabilities. "If September 11, 2001, was a wake-up call," he writes, "clearly America has fallen back asleep." He contends that the government has not budgeted for protecting vital targets (chemical plants, energy facilities, etc.), the private sector has largely ignored security altogether, and the general population has shown an unwillingness to habituate itself to the crisis at hand. Other critics, such as ambassador Charles W. Freeman Jr., suggest that America's unilateral actions, backed by a smug self-assurance, has made the country less attractive to those nations of the world that used to look up to American ideals. Freeman warns that this not only bolsters anti-American sentiment among the nation's enemies but also alienates America's allies from the type of cooperative effort needed to "manage the challenges of national security in the age of terrorism."

On the other end of the spectrum are those who have a more optimistic view of America's success in the current struggle. David Frum and Richard Perle, two members of the American Enterprise Institute, for example, believe that the United States is capable of defeating terrorism and threats from rogue nations if it overcomes the defeatist attitudes of naysayers. The country, they claim, could employ decisive military strokes as well as finely tuned diplomatic pressure if only it were not hobbled by "political and media elite" that are "losing their nerve for the fight." Furthermore, National Security adviser Stephen Hadley attests that the war against America's ideological enemies is as much a war of ideas as a military contest. In redressing terrorism from the Islamic world, Hadley says that "we have some grounds for optimism in this struggle. While our enemies conduct and call for the slaughter of innocents, the overwhelming majority of the Muslim world—along with other civilized peoples everywhere—is increasingly outraged by the atrocities committed in London and Madrid, in Bali and Beslan, in Istanbul and Morocco." Hadley, Frum, and Perle agree that the best weapon the United States has against terrorists and oppressive regimes is the attractiveness of American values and prosperity—and this, they assert, is a powerful weapon that dissuades many from following those who discredit the American way of life.

In *Opposing Viewpoints: National Security*, politicians, government officials, analysts, and commentators debate the security of the nation in the Age of Terrorism. Their arguments are laid out in chapters that address the following pertinent questions: What Are the Most Serious Threats to National Security? How Should the United States Deal with Foreign Nations That Threaten National Security? Are U.S. Homeland Security Measures Effectively Countering Terrorism? How Can U.S. National Security Be Improved? The answers to these questions are fundamentally different than they would have been just a decade ago. America's homeland has already proved vulnerable to attack, and the nation must consider the possibility of further tragedy on American soil. The nation's leaders and advisers are working to limit the risk posed by the Devil's Triangle. The tools of their trade include military action, intelligence gathering, economic pressure, and diplomacy. How the United States chooses to use these assets will define national security policy and, hopefully, keep the country safe from harm.

OPPOSING
VIEWPOINTS®
SERIES

CHAPTER 1

What Are the Most Serious Threats to National Security?

Chapter Preface

In December 2004 President George W. Bush signed into law the Intelligence Reform and Terrorism Prevention Act of 2004. Part of this legislation called for increasing the number of U.S. border patrol agents by 2,000 per year over a five-year period. The intended result was to double the border strength from 10,000 to 20,000 agents by 2010. In 2006, however, the president's budget allowed only for the addition of 210 agents—roughly 10 percent of the proposed increase. Senators quickly tried to add the missing funding to the Department of Homeland Security appropriations bill for 2006. The amendments to secure the funding, however, were defeated in the Senate by a majority of members.

In an editorial to the online magazine *American Chronicle*, Diane M. Grassi claimed, "The Senate's vote epitomized the lack of concern over the largest looming problem in the War on Terrorism in the U.S., which remains the lack of security at U.S. borders." Grassi stated that border patrol authorities estimate that over 3 million illegal aliens entered the United States in 2004 and that only about one in three of those that cross the porous southern U.S. border are captured or turned back. Grassi then reminded her readers that several of the terrorists responsible for the September 11, 2001, tragedies had entered America across the southern border. Other critics of the government's border policies note that lack of detention space has forced border agents to turn loose captive aliens, including Ramzi Yousef, the mastermind behind the 1993 World Trade Center bombing. The lack of holding space and the insufficient number of border patrol agents has many commentators pointing out the irony of carrying out a war against terrorism abroad when the United States cannot seem to secure its own borders.

Government and law enforcement spokespeople, however, are quick to respond that the border situation is not as bleak as supposed. The government has implemented an expedited removal (ER) policy through which border authorities can deport aliens who have entered the United States illegally and cannot prove their presence in the country two weeks prior to their arrest. The U.S. Customs and Border Protection (CBP) agency contends that this measure is primarily directed at the influx of aliens categorized as OTMs (other than Mexicans), a group that in recent years has included Afghanis, Egyptians, Iranians, and Iraqis. The agency also avers that its "defense in depth" strategy is curbing illegal immigration along the U.S-Mexican border. According to this strategy, many types of assets are employed in a zone that only begins at the border and extends into the nation's interior where air reconnaissance and other checkpoints assist in nabbing elusive aliens. In a July 2005 testimony before the House of Representatives, David Aguilar, the chief of the U.S. Border Patrol, stated that "the use of technology, including, the expansion of camera systems, biometrics, sensors, air assets, and improving communications systems can provide the force multiplier that CBP Border Patrol needs to be more effective."

Border security is only one proposed threat to national security in post-9/11 America. In the following chapter, experts discuss other ways in which the United States may be vulnerable to terrorist plots and the actions of unfriendly nations.

> "[The war against terrorism] is a global
> struggle against violent extremism. It
> ... will be long, and it will be hard. I
> wish it were otherwise."

Terrorism Is a Threat to National Security

Donald H. Rumsfeld

In the following viewpoint, former Secretary of Defense Donald H. Rumsfeld addresses U.S. military personnel at the Maxwell-Gunter Air Force Base in Alabama. Rumsfeld tells the assembled men and women that the threat of terrorism against the United States and its allies existed before the September 11, 2001, tragedies and will continue afterward. He maintains that today's extremists are more lethal and fanatical than groups in previous decades. He also argues that their intention is to kill in order to cow nations into submission, and for that purpose, terrorist organizations will seek weapons of mass destruction to make the biggest impression on their enemies. Rumsfeld vows that America will not retreat in the face of terrorist threats, because the causes of freedom and democracy are at stake. Donald H. Rumsfeld stepped down as secretary of defense in November 2006.

Donald H. Rumsfeld, speech delivered at Maxwell-Gunter Air Force Base, Montgomery, Alabama, October 18, 2006. U.S. Department of Defense, www.defenselink.mil.

As you read, consider the following questions:

1. According to Rumsfeld, when has America been accused of taking a "holiday from history"?

2. In the face of global extremist threats, what two options do free societies have, in Rumsfeld's view?

3. How many terrorist plots does the author say have been thwarted by U.S. and allied intelligence agencies since September 11, 2001?

It's now more than five years since we suffered the worst terrorist attack on our soil in history. We came to realize that a war had been declared on our country, on our free people, a war that was certainly not of our making and not of our choosing.

This war was not declared on September 11th, 2001. It really began years, even decades earlier. If you recall, the World Trade Center was attacked by terrorists the first time, not in 2001, but nearly a decade earlier with the bombing in 1993. It was followed by attacks on the Khobar Towers [in Saudi Arabia] in 1996, the embassies in Kenya and Tanzania ... in 1998 and the USS *Cole* just about six years ago [in 2000, when it was attacked by suicide bombers while docked in Yemen].

Yet through it all, many remain persuaded that terrorism was essentially a law-enforcement problem, not an act of war. That terrorists really ought to be treated like criminals—investigated, prosecuted after the fact. The problem is that the folks we're dealing with, the terrorists, are not like bank robbers or common murderers. They're something quite different.

A Problem That Will Not Go Away

People think ... the purpose of terrorism [is] to kill people. It often has that effect. But the purpose of terrorism is not to kill people, it's to terrorize people, it's to alter their behavior, it's to cause them to do something fundamentally different than they otherwise would be doing; that is to say, to do exactly what the terrorists want them to do and to live a life and to behave in a manner consistent with what the terrorists want.

Even as the Cold War ended, our military services remained organized to defend against large armies, air forces and navies. America, it was said, had taken a "holiday from history,"—where Americans were persuaded that emerging threats were exaggerations, or were somebody else's problem, or would eventually go away if we left them alone.

That sentiment was popular in the decades before World War II—until the attack on Pearl Harbor, which awoke many Americans, most Americans, to the harsh reality and caused them to rally to their country's defense, and rally they did. Americans defeated the forces of fascism, nurtured West Germany and Japan on a long, slow, difficult journey to representative government, to democracies, and created new institutions to combat the menace of Soviet tyranny.

The Most Dangerous Enemy

Over the past years, Americans have come to know a new and different threat—an enemy that is even more ruthless and more lethal—as weapons are more lethal today—with no territory to defend, no treaties to honor, that measures progress in terms of decades, not days or weeks or months, as Americans seem to; and who are seeking—let there be no doubt— the world's most dangerous weapons.

With this sort of enemy, we cannot afford and indeed could not survive another "holiday from history." We've seen the nature of the enemy every day since September 11th.

- They target women and children and use them as human shields.

- They've murdered thousands of civilians, tens of thousands—mostly Muslims but non-Muslims alike—in places like London, Madrid, Morocco, Bali, Beslan, Baghdad, New Delhi and dozens of other places across the globe.

- They train their supporters to claim torture when they're apprehended. They manipulate the media.

- They doctor photos of casualties to inflame Western public opinion.

- They seize every opportunity to lie and distort the coalition's missions in Afghanistan, in Iraq and else-where. And they're good at it. They're very skillful at it. They have media committees that meet to decide how they can fool people as to what's taking place.

Going on the Offensive

Their battlefield is not just Baghdad or Kabul, but American living rooms and television screens. We talk about where's the center of gravity of the war. The center of gravity of this war is very much in Washington, D.C., and it's in the capitals across the world.

There's no way our forces can lose, militarily. There's also no way they can win by military means alone. It takes more than military means. And it takes some time.

They live in our country. They live in countries that are our allies in the war on terror. (Some 90 nations today are al-lied with us in the global war on terror.) And they live in dif-fuse cells around the world.

And with an enemy that is not dissuaded by the threat of prosecution or by reason, our free societies have really two options. One is to be terrorized and to alter our behavior, and the other is to decide we will not be terrorized, we'll not alter our behavior, which strikes at the very essence of free people, but to attack them and to stop them at their roots.

Terrorists Exploit Islam

Our terrorist enemies exploit Islam to serve a violent political vision. Fueled by a radical ideology and a false belief that the United States is the cause of most problems affecting Muslims today, our enemies seek to expel Western power and influence from the Muslim world and establish regimes that rule according to a violent and intolerant distortion of Islam. As illustrated by Taliban-ruled Afghanistan, such regimes would deny all political and religious freedoms and serve as sanctuaries for extremists to launch additional attacks against not only the United States, its allies and partners, but the Muslim world itself. Some among the enemy, particularly [the terrorist group] al-Qaida, harbor even greater territorial and geopolitical ambitions and aim to establish a single, pan-Islamic, totalitarian regime that stretches from Spain to Southeast Asia.

This enemy movement seeks to create and exploit a division between the Muslim and non-Muslim world and within the Muslim world itself. The terrorists distort the idea of jihad into a call for violence and murder against those they regard as apostates or unbelievers, including all those who disagree with them. Most of the terrorist attacks since September 11 have occurred in Muslim countries— and most of the victims have been Muslims.

National Security Council, "Today's Terrorist Enemy,"
September 2006.

The government of some 90 nations that we share intelligence with and cooperate with have made the strategic decision to go on the offense, because there really is no other choice. It is not possible to defend in every location, at every moment of the day or night, against every conceivable technique of violence.

That can't be done. So it is a clear choice that one must be on the offense.

Since 9/11, two of the world's leading sponsors of terrorism, the Taliban in Afghanistan and Saddam Hussein's regime in Iraq are gone. A third, Libya, has renounced its nuclear programs and its ties to terror. Nations such as Pakistan and India are much closer allies today than they were in 2001. Some 10 terrorist attacks against America and our allies have been thwarted, to our intelligence community's knowledge. It did not happen by luck. It did not happen by accident.

It happened because an awful lot of people worked very hard to prevent those attacks. It was the result of strategies and the result of close cooperation from a great many other countries.

This war, like other wars, has not been a steady, smooth, upward path. To some, that's a surprise. To those who study history, it is not a surprise. The enemy has a brain. The enemy adapts, just as our folks adapt continuously, and must.

Consider Iraq. At first, Saddam's forces tried to meet Coalition forces in the field—and they lost. So regime remnants and other extremists began to attack military supply convoys. As convoys became better protected, they began to use the [improvised] explosive devices, IEDs. And as commanders shifted convoy tactics and increased armor in response, the type and size of the IEDs changed and the method of actuating them changed. And as the effectiveness of the attacks against military targets declined, the extremists, obviously, using their brains, shifted to more attacks on civilians in attempts to incite sectarian violence. I mean, the classic example was the attack on the Golden Dome Mosque.

Today the enemies are fighting an Iraq unity government by trying to further sow the seeds of sectarian violence. Coalition forces have and will need to continue to adapt, making adjustments as they see the needs.

Each of you here in one form or another is a student of history. You know better than many that what is being undertaken in Afghanistan and Iraq has to be understood to be one of history's most difficult tasks. It is not simply a battle of one big navy against another big navy or one air force against another air force with a signing ceremony on the *Missouri* when it's over.[1] Those are not the kind of people we're dealing with.

Americans Cannot Be Impatient in This War

Afghans have risked their lives to support and defend a representative government that's now been in existence for less than two or three years. Iraqis have given up a great deal to form a unity government, and it's been in place, I don't know, plus or minus 160 days, with the new prime minister and the new ministers—that's less than a baseball season. Think of that. And yet we're impatient. I'm impatient. Everyone's impatient. We can't help but be impatient.

But think of that. That government's been there less than a baseball season. And these are people who lived in that country. And Saddam Hussein did not reward people for being entrepreneurs and taking decisions on their own. Those people were put in jail or killed. They don't have the experience, the base that's needed yet, and it will take some time for them to develop that. To achieve long-term success in this struggle, we're trying to help their governments, their ministries, to offer an alternative of hope and promise for a brighter future. . . .

The overwhelming majority of Afghans and Iraqis do not want a future determined by extremists, by violent extremists, they just don't. Think of it—12 million Iraqis went to vote, and it was dangerous. There were signs on the walls saying, "You vote, you die." They don't want the terrorists to win. They don't want to be turned over to the beheaders and the hostage takers, the terrorists and the 21st-century fascists who seek to do them harm.

1. Japan signed the terms of surrender to end World War II aboard the USS *Missouri*.

The Free World Cannot Retreat Now

This is a global struggle against violent extremism. It is—it will be long, and it will be hard. I wish it were otherwise. They're certainly seeing the violence on television. There's a temptation for people to wonder how will it end, how can it be done in a way that it will end favorably? And of course, as in previous periods, as I have mentioned, there are those who say, "Well, it's somebody else's problem," or "It'll just go away and not to worry."

[Former] British Prime Minister Tony Blair the other day summed up our challenge this way. He said: "We will not win until we shake ourselves free of the wretched capitulation to the propaganda of the enemy that somehow we are the ones responsible. Terrorism is not our fault," he said. "If we retreat now, we will not be safer, we will be committing a craven act of surrender that will put our future security in deepest peril,"

Many of you have experienced first-hand the successes and setbacks of this war. You've witnessed what the enemy is capable of, and I think you know we cannot afford to take a "holiday from history."

Not long ago, a group of men gathered to remember a similar time in history when they were young, when the world's future seemed clouded by the advance of tyrants across the globe.

Those men were volunteers for a mission that seemed foolhardy to some and was very likely to end their lives. But in those famous 30 seconds over Tokyo, the aviators who became known as "Doolittle's Raiders" stunned an empire, rallied a nation, and gave America a needed lift in a world war that at that time we were losing and [that] seemed lost.[2]

It's hard to remember that, but that's what it was. Month after month after month another loss.

2. Only five months after the devastating attack on Pearl Harbor by Japanese forces during World War II, American bomber squadrons under the command of James Doolittle launched a raid against Tokyo in April 1942. Although the bombing caused little damage, the daring act bolstered American morale and demonstrated U.S. power to retaliate.

Those last surviving Doolittle Raiders gave a toast to that past glory, to the legacy they'd forged and to the generations that would carry that legacy into the future. That legacy, that daring, that vision is a hallmark of your service. And I believe I have every confidence that one day you will look back on your service, back on this time, back on your place in history, and take pride in the fact that you contributed to a safer world and to the cause of freedom.

The great sweep of human history is for freedom. And that's the side we're on.

| "The organization that attacked the United States on 9/11 has been shattered and pushed to the brink of extinction."

The Terrorism Threat Is Exaggerated

Robert Dreyfuss

Robert Dreyfuss is a contributing editor to the Nation, *and a frequent political writer for* Mother Jones *and* Rolling Stone. *In the following viewpoint, Dreyfuss argues that the threat of global terrorism has been exaggerated. He claims that al Qaeda, the terrorist organization that carried out the September 11, 2001, attacks on America, has since been devastated and can offer no significant threat. He asserts that various Arab nations are not conspiring with al Qaeda to oppose U.S. interests. Furthermore, he insists that the war in Iraq has nothing to do with fighting terrorism, despite what the White House suggests. Dreyfuss blames the administration of George W. Bush for perpetuating a climate of fear in order to legitimize executive decisions and maintain power over political opponents.*

Robert Dreyfuss, "There Is No War on Terror," *TomPaine.com*, September 13, 2006. Reproduced by permission.

As you read, consider the following questions:

1. According to Carl Ford, as cited by Dreyfuss, why is America willing to overstate the capabilities of al Qaeda?

2. What evidence does Dreyfuss offer to counter the administration's claims that Iraq would fall to terrorists if U.S. forces were to withdraw from that country?

3. In the author's view, how many "serious terrorist plots against the United States" have there been since September 2001?

President George W. Bush, Vice President [Dick] Cheney and the entire Republican election team are scrambling to make their so-called war on terror the focus of the next seven weeks [preceding the 2006 congressional elections]. As in 2002 and 2004, they're counting on their ability to scare Americans with the al-Qaida bogeyman. And while the trauma of 9/11 has begun to dissipate and American voters seem less susceptible than ever to the scare tactics used by the White House, for the past five years the Democrats have been singularly unable to develop an effective counter to the Bush administration on terrorism. So, for that reason, here are 10 important facts about terrorism that opponents of President Bush should understand.

Part of what follows is derived from a series of some two dozen interviews I conducted over the summer with leading U.S. counterterrorism officials, many of whom served in top posts during the Bush administration. Not all of them agree with each other, nor with all of my conclusions, which "can be found" in the Sept. 21 [2006] issue of *Rolling Stone*. But most of them served on the front lines of the so-called "war on terror." If U.S. counterterrorism efforts were run by these officials, instead of Bush and Cheney, those efforts would look radically different than they do today.

The Threat of Terrorism
Is Wildly Exaggerated

A strong and convincing case that the al-Qaida bogeyman is inflated far beyond the real but limited threat that it poses is made in the current issue of *Foreign Affairs*, in "an article" by political scientist John Mueller. He and others argue persuasively that the reason the United States has not been attacked since 9/11 is that terrorists are far less powerful than the White House claims. "If al Qaeda operatives are as determined and inventive as assumed, they should be here by now. If they are not yet here, they must not be trying very hard or must be far less dedicated, diabolical, and competent than the common image would suggest," writes Mueller. Why haven't the Democrats picked up this argument?

Al-Qaida Barely Exists at All as a Threat

The organization that attacked the United States on 9/11 has been shattered and pushed to the brink of extinction, despite claims to the contrary of the vast anti-terrorism industrial complex and its journalistic heavy-breathers. I interviewed Carl Ford, the former assistant secretary of state for intelligence, who told me:

> We're overstating their capability, because we can't believe that there isn't a more nefarious explanation for the fact that we haven't been attacked. There aren't a lot of terrorists out there, and they're not 10-feet tall. . . . One appealing hypothesis is: they've been damaged more than we know.

The Democrats should stop ringing alarm bells about al-Qaida and explain calmly that the terrorist threat, which was small [in 2001], has been greatly reduced since 9/11.

There Is No Terrorist International

President Bush lumps the remnants of al-Qaida together with states such as Iran and Syria, the resistance movement in Iraq, insurgent political parties such as Hezbollah and Hamas and

Achieving Victory

My fellow Americans, we have achieved something almost no one thought possible [in 2001]. The nation did not suffer the quick follow-up attacks so many people feared and expected. Our troops found the people who were responsible for the worst attack ever on our soil. We killed many, we captured more, and we placed their leaders in a position where they could not direct the next despicable attack on our people—and where the conscience of the world's people, of whatever faith, has turned against them for their barbarism. They have been a shame to their own great faith, and to all other historic standards of decency.

Achieving this victory does not mean the end of threats. Life is never free of dangers. I wish I could tell you that no American will ever again be killed or wounded by a terrorist—and that no other person on this earth will be either. But I cannot say that, and you could not believe me if I did. Life brings risk—especially life in an open society, like the one that people of this land have sacrificed for centuries to create.

James Fallows, Atlantic, *September 2006.*

other assorted entities into one, big "Islamofascist" enemy. Nothing could be more ill-informed or further from the truth. "That's an oversimplification of the task of dealing with the tactic [terrorism] that is used by many different groups, with many different ideologies," Paul R. Pillar, a former top CIA [Central Intelligence Agency] analyst and the author of a respected book on terrorism, told *The Washington Post.* "It leads to a misunderstanding of the need of what is in fact a different counterterrorist policy for each group and state we are dealing with. . . . Hamas is an entirely different entity than al-Qaeda. . . . Their objectives are very much different." Pillar said much the same thing to me. Bush claims that al-Qaida and its terrorist allies want to create an "empire that spans from Spain to Indonesia." Not a chance. Larry Wilkerson, the former top aide to [former secretary of state] Colin Powell, told me: "I don't think there's a soul in the administration, except for Vice President Dick Cheney, who believes that crap about Islamofascism." Why don't Democrats ridicule this specific sort of fear-mongering?

Iraq Will Not, and Could Not, Fall to al-Qaida

The Iraqi resistance is overwhelmingly made up of Sunni, former Baathist, nationalist members of Iraq's former military and intelligence services, Sunni tribal leaders and just plain old "pissed-off Iraqis." It is not al-Qaida. When Bush says that by leaving Iraq we would turn Iraq over to the al-Qaida types, he is making the same false argument that he made [in 2001]. Then, he told us that Saddam Hussein backed Osama bin Laden. Now, he tells us that pro–Saddam Hussein Iraqis back pro–bin Laden al-Qaida types. He lied then and he is lying now.

The Taliban Is Not al-Qaida

In 2001, the Taliban and al-Qaida may have had a marriage of convenience. But, as in many marriages, it was not a happy one. Mullah Omar and the Taliban leadership were suspicious and resentful of al-Qaida, and some Taliban leaders were openly hostile to bin Laden. Today, the resurgence of the Taliban in Afghanistan is a sad reminder that Bush bungled Afghanistan, too—but the Taliban fighters are Afghan Islamists, like the *mujahideen* that the CIA supported in the 1980s. They are not Arabs or foreign fighters, and they are not al-Qaida. If the Taliban pose a threat to U.S. interests, it is not a terrorist one.

Neither Iran nor Syria Sponsor Anti-U.S. Terrorism

Al-Qaida has zero support in Iran and Syria. The Syrian regime is fiercely hostile to al-Qaida-style fundamentalist Islam. Iran, a Shiite theocracy, is bitterly hostile to Sunni fundamentalism and to al-Qaida. Although both countries tactically support Hamas and Hezbollah against Israel and although Iran routinely assassinates opposition leaders abroad, neither country has attacked the United States in decades. The few al-Qaida leaders—including Osama bin Laden's son—reported to be in Iran are under house arrest and do not lead operations for the shattered terrorist group. Yet that hasn't stopped Bush administration officials, such as Nicholas Burns of the State Department, from accusing Iran of "harboring" al-Qaida. Nonsense.

It Is Not a "War"

Although the Pentagon has garnered 90 percent of the money for the so-called war on terrorism, and although the Pentagon's special operations command is supposedly in charge of the "war," it is not a war. Terrorism cannot be fought with tanks, planes and missiles. The Defense Department cannot invade the London suburbs or mosques in Hamburg [Germany] or the teeming cities of Pakistan. Cells of angry Muslims will coalesce spontaneously to seek revenge for real or alleged wrongs for decades to come. That is a problem for the CIA, the FBI, and, especially, foreign police and intelligence services, not [former secretary of defense] Donald Rumsfeld's legions. "I hate the term 'global war on terrorism,'" John O. Brennan, who headed the National Counterterrorism Center until [2005], told me. "The Department of Defense and others insist very strongly on calling it a war, because that allows the Pentagon to prosecute the military dimension of the conflict. It fits their strategy."

There Were Never Any al-Qaida Sleeper Cells in the United States

In 2002, the Bush administration leaked to the press its assertion that al-Qaida had 5,000 "sleepers" in the United States, dormant agents that could be activated by Osama bin Laden. There were none—at least, not a single one has been found, and no terrorism has occurred [since 9/11]. No terrorism at all: [Since 9/11], no one in the United States has as much as been punched in the nose by an angry Muslim fundamentalist.

Vulnerabilities Are Not Threats

The unnecessary, superfluous Department of Homeland Security [DHS] is tracking countless points of vulnerability. Trains and trucks, buses and subways, chemical plants and factories, airports and [sea]ports, skyscrapers and bridges, tunnels and dams—the list of potential targets is endless. But the list of potential terrorists is infinitesimally small. Despite the recently uncovered London plot [involving an alleged plan to explode bombs aboard airplanes]—details of which have still not been revealed and which is increasingly looking exaggerated—there hasn't even been a single advanced terrorist plot uncovered in the United States since 9/11. President Bush gamely cites 10 supposed plots stopped by U.S. counterterrorism efforts, but on closer examination all 10 are either bogus or were to take place overseas. According to several top counterterrorism officials, the number of serious terrorist plots against the United States [since 2001] is: zero.

No One Is in Charge

After the creation of the DHS, the Office of the Director of National Intelligence, the National Counterterrorism Center, the U.S. Northern Command, the FBI's new intelligence division and other counterterrorism agencies, no one is in charge. "We have a more confusing organization now," Pillar told me.

"It's really hard to answer the question 'Who's in charge?'" Every agency, from the Pentagon to the lowliest police department, has used the threat of terrorism to win ever-larger appropriations from federal, state and local governments for the ostensible purpose of fighting terrorism. So far, none of them have found any actual terrorists—but the proliferation of competing agencies continues, and they continue to step on each other's toes.

After 9/11, the Bush administration launched an open-ended war on an ambiguous enemy ("terror") while offering the nation no definition of what victory would look like. Five years later [in 2006], the nation has spent billions in taxpayer dollars and lost thousands of American lives fighting a threat that should be the province of law enforcement and intelligence services, not the military. And the White House tells us there is no end in sight.

"The threat posed by the proliferation of weapons of mass destruction is the number one national security threat facing our country."

Weapons of Mass Destruction Are a Threat to National Security

Richard G. Lugar

Richard G. Lugar states in the following viewpoint that weapons of mass destruction are the primary security threat to the United States. Lugar contends that these weapons—either left over from Cold War stockpiles or produced from newer technologies—are within reach of America's enemies. In addition, he claims that with such weapons, a relatively small group of fanatics could cripple the normal functioning of the United States and injure or kill unprecedented numbers of Americans. For these reasons, Lugar asserts that America must secure foreign stockpiles and work with the international community to prevent proliferation. Richard G. Lugar is a U.S. senator from Indiana, and his views presented here are excerpted from a speech delivered to Congress in 2005.

Richard G. Lugar, "Lugar Commends the Certification of the Indiana Weapons of Mass Destruction Civil Support Team," December 13, 2005. http://lugar.senate.gov.

As you read, consider the following questions:

1. As Lugar states, what rebel group detonated a radiological weapon in Moscow in 1995?

2. Besides weapons themselves, what other two resources from the former Soviet Union might current enemies of the United States exploit to help build weapons of mass destruction, in the author's opinion?

3. As Lugar explains, what are Project Sapphire and Operation Auburn Endeavor?

I rise today [December 13, 2005] to commend the certification of the Indiana Civil Support Team [CST] and the support it will provide the people of Indiana in the event of an attack utilizing a weapon of mass destruction [WMD]. . . . Many prefer not to think of the horrors associated with nuclear, chemical and biological weapons, but the 22 members of the 53rd WMD-CST don't have that luxury. It is their job to help protect Hoosiers should a WMD attack occur in Indiana.

On November 28, 2005, the Pentagon announced that the Indiana Civil Support Team was fully ready to assist civil authorities in responding to a domestic weapon of mass destruction incident. . . .

America Should Be More Worried

[That] announcement occurred with little fanfare and negligible public interest. This is unfortunate because the threat posed by the proliferation of weapons of mass destruction is the number one national security threat facing our country.

Chemical weapons were introduced on the battlefields of World War I. Nuclear weapons ended World War II. Biological weapons were components of Cold War arsenals. The 20th century witnessed the brutal use of these powerful weapons by superpowers and nation-states. Technological advancements and the proliferation of weapons, materials and know-how have made weapons of mass destruction accessible to a growing number of national and non-state entities.

Despite the threat of nuclear annihilation throughout the standoff between the U.S. and the Soviet Union, it was unfathomable that a religious sect could acquire the means to attack a major metropolitan subway system with biological weapons. Yet, the Aum Shinrikyo dispersed anthrax in a Tokyo train station in March 1995. Who would have expected rebels from a remote region of the Caucasus to threaten the detonation of a radiological weapon in a Moscow park. Chechens did that in November 1995. Even more difficult to believe would have been the notion that the leader of a deadly terrorist organization would announce that it was the organization's mission to acquire a weapon of mass destruction and use it against the United States. Osama bin Laden did that in December 1998.

The use of a weapon of mass destruction in the United States could cripple our economy, lead to the fall of our government, and threaten large segments of our population with disease and death. During the Cold War, the Soviet Union had the resources and incentives to carefully guard and maintain these weapons and the scientific knowledge that produced them. But the political collapse of the Moscow government was accompanied by a broader economic collapse throughout the vast nation. Not only did Russia and the other successor states have few resources for maintaining the Soviet-era arsenal, they could not even afford to adequately pay members of the military and scientific community who had responsibility for safeguarding the weapons and related technology. The United States faced the grim possibility that weapons previously held in impenetrable Soviet facilities and technology previously restricted to the minds and computers of elite Soviet scientists could be stolen or sold to the highest bidder.

The Spread of Destructive Knowledge

[Oklahoma City bomber Timothy] McVeigh's fertilizer bomb may seem quaint compared to the post-9/11 anthrax or the nuclear materials we fear Al Qaeda has, but it falls into their lineage once you reduce all three to their basic source: growing ingenuity in the concoction of lethal force; wider availability of the ingredients in an ever-more-industrialized, interconnected world; and growing access, via information technology, to the knowledge needed to use them.

Of course, Osama [bin Laden]–era [i.e., post-9/11] technologies are more menacing than McVeigh-era technologies. That's the point. What today's Internet is to shortwave radio and mailed videotapes, tomorrow's Internet will be to today's. As streaming video penetrates the most remote parts of the world, every Web-cam-equipped terro-vangelist will have global reach. And information technologies, like the advancing weapons technologies whose use they make more likely, are equal-opportunity empowerers.

Robert Wright, New York Times, *April 26, 2005.*

Extremist Threats

As a country, we must acknowledge that the weapons that haunted the Cold War are now available to irrational and un-deterrable foes. While the threat of nuclear attack from the Soviet Union was awesome, it was certain, in that we knew who and where our enemy was and had the ability to hold them at equal peril. The post–Cold War security environment is anything but certain. Battles are no longer determined by armored divisions taking and holding large swaths of territory. Nor is strategic competition marked by the building of the biggest bomb or the longest-range missiles. A small group of fanatics with the right contacts and resources can obtain and utilize a weapon of mass destruction that could destroy or make unlivable large portions of Washington D.C., New York, or Chicago. Similarly, toxins introduced into our food supply and distribution systems could spread disease and panic.

There is no silver bullet to these threats. U.S. security will be secured by small numbers of American government officials and contractors working with former enemies to eliminate the weapons that could threaten the future of our country. It will also depend on American allies working closely and effectively in detecting and interdicting these weapons and local police officers, medical personnel, and guardsmen preparing to respond to a WMD event.

Since the end of the Cold War, I have worked with colleagues here in Congress and the Executive Branch to defend the American people from these threats. I have often described the best strategy to deal with the WMD threat as "defense-in-depth," layers of defensive efforts designed to stop a nuclear, chemical and biological weapon from reaching our shores.

The first line of defense is prevention and entails activities at the source to stop weapons, materials and know-how from leaving their current locations. The second is detection and interdiction and involves efforts to stem the flow of illicit trade in these weapons and materials at foreign and domestic borders. The third line of defense is crisis and consequence management and requires domestic preparedness should such threats turn into hostile acts. Individually, each of these lines of defense is insufficient; together, they help to form the policy fabric of an integrated defense-in-depth.

The Nunn-Lugar Program

In 1991, I joined with Senator Sam Nunn and co-authored the Nunn-Lugar Cooperative Threat Reduction Program. The program's goal is to address the threat posed by nuclear, chemical and biological weapons at their source. Over the program's first decade and a half it has focused on the threats emanating from the former Soviet Union. When the USSR crumbled it had the largest nuclear, chemical and biological arsenals in the world. The next day four new independent countries emerged from the ashes with nuclear weapons. The totalitarian command and control system that secured the chemical and biological weapons arsenals and infrastructure disappeared. Divisions of ballistic missiles, wings of long-range bombers, and fleets of strategic missile submarines were left with a bankrupt, dysfunctional master and numerous in-dividuals and organizations seeking to steal them.

The Nunn-Lugar Program has made excellent progress in eliminating these threats. Ukraine, Belarus, and Kazakhstan emerged as the third, fourth and eighth largest nuclear powers in the world. Today all three are nuclear weapons free. More than 6,760 nuclear warheads, each capable of destroying an American city, have been deactivated. Nearly 2,000 interconti-nental ballistic missiles fired from land-based silos, missile submarines, and bombers have been eliminated. Two-thirds of the Soviet Union's strategic bomber force and over half of its strategic submarine force have been destroyed.

The Soviet Union also left behind enormous quantities of chemical and biological weapons materials. Russia declared a chemical weapons stockpile of 40,000 metric tons stored un-der questionable [security]. A public accounting of the Soviet biological weapons programs has never been made, but it is believed to be the largest and most advanced in the world. Tens of thousands of scientists, engineers, and technicians had assisted in the development of the Soviet Union's weapons of mass destruction. With the economies of Russia and other re-publics in bad shape, many of these experts faced unemploy-ment and concerns existed that they might have an incentive to sell their skills to other countries and terrorist organiza-tions. In each of these cases, Nunn-Lugar has responded with innovative dismantlement strategy for the chemical weapons stocks, elimination of biological weapons production capacity and security upgrades for pathogen collections, and partnering with the private sector to find long-term, peaceful employment for former weapons experts.

Nunn-Lugar has also taken on formerly top-secret missions to remove dangerous weapons and materials before they could fall into the wrong hands. In November 1994, the U.S. launched Project Sapphire to remove 600 kilograms of highly enriched uranium [HEU] from Kazakhstan and ship it to Oak Ridge, Tennessee. More recently, Operation Auburn Endeavor was carried out in Georgia to remove HEU and transport it to Scotland. In Moldova, the U.S. removed fourteen MiG-29s [airplanes] capable of launching nuclear weapons because of efforts by a number of rogue states to acquire them.

Despite the progress we made in the former Soviet Union, the skills and capabilities of the Nunn-Lugar Program were confined to that geographical region. In 2004, Congress changed that by approving the Nunn-Lugar Expansion Act which authorized the use of up to $50 million in Nunn-Lugar funds for activities outside the former Soviet Union. This authority will be used for the first time in Albania to destroy nearly 16 tons of chemical weapons and consideration is being given for the program to work in Libya and countries in Southeast Asia. . . .

Over the last fifteen years, I have worked closely with both [the George H.W. and George W.] Bush Administrations and President [Bill] Clinton to safeguard the American people from the threats associated with weapons of mass destruction. We still have much work to do, but the certification of the Indiana WMD-CST makes the people of Indiana safer. I am thankful that in the event of a WMD incident the people of Indiana will not be alone, local first responders and the WMD-CST will be there to provide assistance and expertise.

> "Despite all of the government hoopla surrounding weapons of mass destruction prior to and subsequent to September 11, the threat has been hyped."

The Weapons of Mass Destruction Threat Is Exaggerated

Ivan Eland

Ivan Eland is the director of the Center for Peace at the Independent Institute. He holds a PhD in national security policy from the George Washington University. In the following viewpoint, Eland states that U.S. government propaganda has hyped the threat of weapons of mass destruction (WMD). Eland contends that such weapons are hard to manufacture, difficult to deliver, and any nation using them would incur the swift retribution of the United States. Furthermore, Eland says that rogue nations with WMD capabilities would not hand them over to terrorist groups for fear that American intelligence would trace them back to their source.

Ivan Eland, "Weapons of Mass Destruction Are Overrated As a Threat to America," The Independent Institute, January 28, 2004. www.independent.org. Reproduced by permission of The Independent Institute, 100 Swan Way, Oakland, CA 94621-1428 USA.

45

As you read, consider the following questions:

1. Why does Eland think that only nuclear weapons should be categorized as weapons of mass destruction?

2. In the author's opinion, what does the success of biological or chemical attacks depend on?

3. What strategy does Eland suggest will work best for containing nations with nuclear weapons?

David Kay, the president's handpicked weapons of mass destruction snoop in Iraq, has resigned and criticized U.S. intelligence for not realizing that Iraqi weapons programs were in disarray. He now thinks that the stocks of chemical and biological weapons were destroyed in the 1990s—out of fear that U.N. weapons inspectors would discover them—and that new production was not initiated. He also believes that Iraq's nuclear program had been restarted but was only at a very primitive stage—hardly the imminent threat alleged by the [George W.] Bush administration as a justification for immediate war. So with the final nail being driven into the coffin of the administration's main rationale for war against Iraq, Iraqi weapons programs are not the only things in disarray. After Kay's initial comments, Secretary of State Colin Powell had to admit that the Iraqi government may no longer have had such arms.

A Hyped Threat

Perhaps Kay's findings will finally cause the American public to heed the Iraq war critics' call to hold the administration accountable for the deaths of more than 500 American service personnel and countless innocent Iraqis (which, strangely, the American government cannot seem to estimate). But let's not hold our breath. The September 11 tragedy gave the Bush administration body armor that is only now developing chinks. And Kay's findings help debunk the Iraqi threat but may actually cloud other issues. First, Kay blames U.S. intelligence for not realizing that Iraq's weapons programs were in shambles. This conclusion is valid, but fits into the administration's desire to scapegoat U.S. spy agencies to hide its own twisting and embellishing of the already faulty intelligence information.

Second and important to remember during propaganda campaigns preceding any future invasions of "axis of evil" nations: despite all of the government hoopla surrounding weapons of mass destruction prior to and subsequent to September 11, the threat has been hyped. Prior to the invasion of Iraq, the Department of Defense noted "extant and emerging threats" from 12 nations with nuclear programs, 13 countries with biological weapons, and 16 nations with chemical weapons.

Although nuclear, chemical and biological weapons usually fall under the scary (it's done on purpose) WMD label, only nuclear weapons should be in that category. (As the September 11 attacks showed, high casualties could be inflicted without using WMD.) Chemical weapons have a much smaller area of contamination than do biological and nuclear arms and historically have been less deadly than even conventional bombs. Chemical weapons are best employed by the defending side—if the attacking side uses them, friendly troops would likely have to advance through the gas. Although chemical weapons are probably the easiest of the three to produce, [the terrorist group] al Qaeda's efforts to date have been very crude. Some infrastructure is needed to produce chemical weapons so detection of production may be possible.

Difficult Weapons to Make

Although biological weapons are better for terrorizing civilian populations than for battlefield use (they take effect slowly and the battle probably will be over by then), weaponizing biological agents takes a great deal of scientific expertise. Aum Shinrikyo, a well-funded Japanese terror group, hired scien-

State	Nuclear	Chemical	Biological
Albania		Declared	
China	Declared	Suspected	Suspected
Egypt		Suspected	Suspected
France	Declared		
India	Declared	Declared	
Iran		Suspected	Suspected
Israel	Declared	Suspected	Suspected
Libya		Declared	
North Korea	Declared*	Suspected	Suspected
Pakistan	Declared		
Russia	Declared	Declared	Suspected
South Korea		Declared	
Syria		Suspected	
UK	Declared		
US	Declared	Declared	

States with Declared or Suspected Weapons of Mass Destruction

*In October 2006, North Korea announced it had conducted a nuclear test detonation. The blast was so small that some nations question the success of the test.

TAKEN FROM: Carnegie Endowment for International Peace, "Proliferation Status 2005 Map." www.proliferationnews.org. Updated to include North Korea's nuclear test in October 2006.

tists to do so but was unsuccessful. Although small pox could cause casualties on the scale of a nuclear detonation, only a few countries have the virus. A successful attack with either chemical or biological weapons is heavily dependent on favorable weather conditions. Missiles are not the ideal delivery systems for either type of weapon because the agent can be incinerated by heat from the explosive impact.

No one would argue that nuclear weapons are incapable of causing mass destruction. But building nuclear weapons requires a large infrastructure, scientists, engineers and strictly controlled fissile material (plutonium or enriched uranium).

Terrorists are probably not capable of building even a crude nuclear weapon. Many countries aren't either. Iraq and Libya both failed to get such weapons.

Deterrence Works

But some clearly undesirable governments—for example, North Korea—eventually may get nuclear weapons and the long-range missiles to deliver them to the United States.[1] North Korea always has been a bigger WMD [weapons of mass destruction] threat than Iraq. But the United States could rely on its world dominant nuclear arsenal to deter attacks from the small arsenals of nascent nuclear powers, rather than conducting unnecessary preventative invasions. The United States took this route when the totalitarian Soviet Union and the even more radical Maoist China were developing nuclear weapons. Deterrence has worked in the past and will most likely work in the future because the remaining destitute "rogue" states have home addresses that could be wiped off the map—albeit with massive casualties—with thousands of U.S. nuclear warheads. Moreover, even though those nations disagree with intrusive U.S. foreign policy in their regions, they have no incentive to give such costly weapons to unpredictable terrorist groups. If such assistance were discovered, the superpower might be motivated to incinerate their countries. Before the war, the president's own CIA [Central Intelligence Agency] reported that Iraq would be unlikely to use WMD or give them to terrorists unless the United States invaded.

Although the unnecessary and continuing deaths of Americans and Iraqis are tragic, most alarming for the republic may have been the absence of public outcry to halt the administration's rush into a war that its own intelligence agency predicted would be counterproductive.

1. In 2006, North Korea claimed to have successfully detonated a nuclear weapon. The recorded blast was so small that some nations question the success of the test.

"We are now less likely to be attacked by
international terrorists than by homegrown American citizens."

Homegrown Terrorists Are a Threat to National Security

Mortimer B. Zuckerman

*In the following viewpoint, Mortimer B. Zuckerman states that
threats in the age of terrorism do not always come from foreign
countries. Zuckerman argues that the Internet has given Muslim
jihadists (holy warriors) in the United States and other free nations the information needed to construct bombs and carry out
terrorist plots. He fears that Americans especially may be too focused on Iraq and other supposed centers of terrorist activities to
recognize the dangers posed by militant Muslim groups within
the United States. Unless law enforcement finds a means of un-
covering homegrown terrorists, Zuckerman asserts, America may
pay the price of its inattention. Mortimer B. Zuckerman is the
chairman and editor in chief of* U.S. News & World Report *and
is the publisher of the New York* Daily News.

As you read, consider the following questions:

1. As Zuckerman notes, how many terrorist plots have British intelligence authorities stopped to date?

2. What dangerous skills and practices does Zuckerman say homegrown terrorists can learn off the Internet?

3. What does Zuckerman think about the loss of civil liberties that may come from implementing new methods of law enforcement aimed at catching terrorists?

It is chilling that the [congressionally authorized] Baker-Hamilton report [which in part calls for the withdrawal of troops from Iraq] came on the eve of Pearl Harbor's anniversary. In 1941, clashes every day in the Atlantic Ocean made us more focused on the imminence of war with Germany than with Japan. Today all eyes are on Iraq. It's called the center of the war on terrorism, but it must not monopolize our attention. We need a third eye because we are now less likely to be attacked by international terrorists than by homegrown American citizens, self-radicalized individuals who are members of groups inspired by al Qaeda [the perpetrators of the September 11, 2001, attacks on America] propaganda.

This is a profoundly demoralizing thought, given the long tradition of success our nation has enjoyed in infusing newcomers with the American ideal. Britain, taking a different course, was proud to have created a multicultural society. But apparently well-adapted young Muslims who were born in Britain exploded the subway bombs of July 2005. Now the head of Britain's domestic intelligence agency, Eliza Manningham-Buller, has come out with a grave warning. Not so long ago it was an offense for anyone even to mention the name of the head of [the United Kingdom's Security Agency] MI-5. (The box office hit, *Casino Royale*, has it right: 007's boss, Judi Dench, is a distinctly anonymous figure.) So the fact that the MI-5 director has stepped out of the shadows is significant in itself. And what she says is that there are many

Response of the American Muslim Community

By and large, American Muslims express great concern over the prospect of homegrown terrorists in their midst. To this end, members of Islamic communities have worked to establish good relationships with U.S. officials, particularly on the local level. Hussein Ibish, executive director of the Hala Salaam Maksoud Foundation for Arab-American Leadership, says [that] in terms of counterterrorism efforts, "most of the major successes the government claims within the United States have actually involved cooperation with the local Muslim communities." He points to the arrest of the "Lackawanna Six," a group of Yemeni-Americans who attended a terrorist training camp in Afghanistan, as one example where reports of suspicion from Muslims in the area led to the initial government investigation.

Eben Kaplan, "American Muslims and the Threat of Homegrown Terrorism," CFR.org, September 22, 2006. Reproduced by permission.

more British Muslims who back the terrorists. MI-5 has stopped five plots to date. We know of the one to blow up 10 planes over the Atlantic, but MI-5 is monitoring 1,600 other suspects, mostly homegrown Islamic terrorists who get their training in murder and mayhem on the Internet. In Germany, too, only an alert train conductor prevented the detonation of propane and gasoline bombs that would have horribly burned and killed hundreds of commuters.

A New Training Ground

Interviews with the heads of counterterrorism and local police officials in the United States yield similar assessments. The threat is from second- and third-generation children of immigrants, fluent in English and accustomed to American society but using the legal rights of U.S. citizenship to rebel from within. They have learned the Koran on the Internet; they lead small clusters of 20 to 25 mostly young men who share feelings of alienation, a longing for self-importance, a need to be a part of some larger group or cause. They have developed what is called "adversarial assimilation."

The Internet has replaced Afghanistan as a training ground. It is effectively the university of jihadist studies, where hundreds of Muslims from all corners of the world can study the rules of jihad, while they live in it anonymously. Here they learn to fire a shoulder-held antiaircraft missile; to prepare explosives and make bombs out of batteries and improvise hand-thrown charges to hit vehicles; to seek a position on a crowded bus to achieve maximum casualties; to plan kidnappings; and to concoct botulism toxin.

Marc Sageman, who collected the life histories of 400 would-be jihadists, found that most were well-to-do, with two thirds having some college education and only 27 percent characterized as lower class. Some 70 percent joined the ranks of the global jihadists while away from home. Separated from the traditional bonds of family and culture, they drifted to the mosques more for companionship than for religion, but there they found extremists who appeared to offer a compelling, all-encompassing explanation for their feelings of anomie and lack of self-worth.

In Need of a New Way to Fight Terrorists

If we are to avert mass casualties from the enemies within, it is imperative to fashion a new approach to find these people. Our criminal justice model has been to look for the criminal after the crime. This won't do any longer. How do you punish a suicide bomber? We must disrupt plots before they are carried out. Gathering this intelligence will impinge on traditional civil liberties, but we simply don't have much choice. As the well-known journalist, Harold Evans, told the Hudson In-

stitute recently, "I'd rather be photographed by a hidden surveillance camera than travel on a train with men carrying
bombs in their backpack. I'd regard being blown to bits on
the street as more of an intrusion of privacy than having an
identity card."

The jihadists are not just another protest group. They recognize no moral and legal standards—and we are fighting
them with one hand behind our backs: The sad fact is that
over the years our government has not earned enough trust to
allow for reasonable compromises by which the intelligence
agencies could get the bad guys without violating the privacy
of the good guys.

What has been done to date—border controls, intensity of
interrogation, even airport searches—has not diminished most
citizens' "feel of freedom." But if we were to experience a major attack that could have been thwarted by effective countermeasures, the public outcry for action would make the present
restrictions seem a mere bagatelle. So the greatest threat to
civil liberties today is not preventive measures, but failing to
take them.

"The lethal threat from terrorism . . . cannot be separated from our reliance on foreign oil."

Dependence on Foreign Oil Is a Threat to National Security

Michael T. Klare

In the following viewpoint, Michael T. Klare argues that the United States is dependent on foreign oil reserves in countries that are unstable and that harbor growing anti-American sentiment. If these nations should experience a crisis that cuts off oil delivery, the U.S. economy and national security, Klare fears, would be compromised. Michael T. Klare is a professor of peace and world security studies at Hampshire College in Amherst, Massachusetts. He is also the author of Resource Wars: The New Landscape of Global Conflict.

As you read, consider the following questions:

1. What percentage of the world's oil reserves are located in the Middle East, according to Klare?

2. In Klare's view, why are oil-pumping facilities and transport lines in the Middle East legitimate targets to anti-American factions in this region?

Michael T. Klare, "Oil: The Real Threat to National Security," *Salon.com*, October 4, 2004. This article first appeared in *Salon.com*, at www.salon.com. An online version remains in the *Salon.com* archives. Reprinted with permission.

3. On what does Klare place the chief blame for America's high rate of oil consumption?

As the [2004] presidential campaign draws to a close, the two major candidates [George W. Bush and John Kerry] are sparring over many aspects of American foreign policy—notably Iraq, the war on terrorism, and America's fraying ties with other major powers. But there is one critical topic that both are refusing to confront frankly: America's growing dependence on imported petroleum.

Rising oil dependency has many serious consequences for the United States. To begin with, it entails a mammoth transfer of national wealth to foreign oil producers: nearly $200 billion per year at current prices. These transfers represent the single largest contribution to our staggering balance-of-payments deficit and are steadily eroding the value of the dollar. Growing dependency also compels us to coddle foreign oil potentates like the royal family of Saudi Arabia—some of whose members made lavish donations to Islamic charities linked to [terrorist leader] Osama bin Laden and al-Qaida. Worst of all, our dependence renders us highly vulnerable to oil shocks caused by turmoil and conflict in the major producing areas abroad.

The High Stakes of Oil Dependence

These are not new concerns. The United States has been exposed to the fallout of rising oil dependency for some time. But the severity of the problem has become more pronounced over the past few years. As the United States has deepened its reliance on imported petroleum, the center of gravity of world oil production has shifted inexorably from established producers in the industrialized world to emerging suppliers in the Middle East, Africa, and the Andean region of Latin America—war zones all. The further we look into the future, therefore, the greater the risk of international oil crises.

Given the high stakes involved, oil dependency should be among the top issues discussed in the campaign. Both major candidates should be offering detailed plans for reducing our reliance on imports and developing alternative sources of energy. And, to be fair, both have made token statements in this direction: Sen. Kerry has called for greater spending on petroleum alternatives, while President Bush has touted his plan to promote energy "independence" by drilling in Alaska and other protected wilderness areas. But neither candidate has been willing to face the fact that American dependence on imported oil will continue to grow unless we adopt far more ambitious plans of conservation and changes in technology.

The reluctance to contemplate such moves is understandable. The American economy is deeply dependent on cheap and abundant petroleum, and more and more of that energy must be acquired from foreign suppliers. Even if Alaska's Arctic National Wildlife Refuge [ANWR] actually contains all the oil it is said to possess—about 10 billion barrels—we would still be dependent on imports for an ever-growing share of our energy needs. Even the production of more hybrid vehicles will not make a real dent in our foreign oil consumption, so long as most Americans continue to drive the relatively inefficient vehicles now on the road. As things stand now, we are destined to be even more beholden to foreign producers in the future than we are at present.

A Volatile Part of the World

The fact that we have become so dependent on imported oil is scary enough. But what is truly frightening is that an ever-increasing share of our imported energy will come from countries that are chronically unstable, torn by ethnic and religious conflict, or [that] house anti-American terrorists—or some combination of all three. The ever-turbulent Middle East harbors 65 percent of the world's known oil reserves, while producers in Africa, Latin America and Asia possess another 20

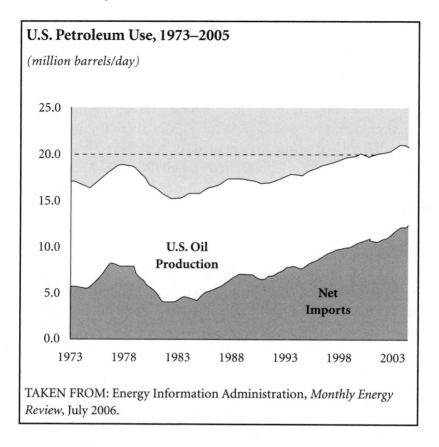

U.S. Petroleum Use, 1973–2005

(million barrels/day)

TAKEN FROM: Energy Information Administration, *Monthly Energy Review*, July 2006.

percent. These countries or their self-appointed rulers may want to sell us their petroleum, but they lack the capacity to maintain stability in their own territory and so cannot always guarantee a safe and reliable stream of crude. As a result, supplies are curtailed, prices rise and the global economy is at risk of a slowdown or contraction—precisely the conditions we face today.

This is not a temporary worry. We may get past the current upheavals in Iraq, Nigeria and Venezuela and see lower energy prices in the year ahead. But even if these key suppliers settle down a bit, others—Iran, Saudi Arabia, Angola, Azerbaijan—are likely to become more restive. There simply is no escape from oil-supply disruptions and the resulting economic traumas produced by instability in producing regions abroad.

The propensity toward violence in these areas is partly a result of the historic antagonisms that plague many of these countries—Shiites versus Sunnis, Arabs versus Persians, Muslims versus Christians and so on. Even without petroleum, these countries would be subject to periodic upheavals. But the discovery and production of oil tends to exacerbate these differences, bringing immense wealth to some and disappointment to others—a sure source of conflict. In Nigeria, for example, the dominant tribes of the north have largely monopolized the allocation of national oil revenues, while the marginalized tribes of the south—where most of the oil is produced—have been excluded from these benefits. The unsurprising result: tribes in the south are threatening civil war and a costly oil-production shutdown unless the government channels more petroleum wealth to their impoverished communities.

Terrorist Targets

But this is only part of the problem. Many of these countries were once occupied or controlled by the major colonial powers, and so harbor deep resentments toward any remnant or reminder of colonialism. As the leading Western power, the United States has become a magnet for much of this wrath. And because the most visible expressions of American involvement in these countries are the large U.S.-based energy firms, anything to do with oil—pipelines, pumping stations, refineries, tankers and so on—becomes a legitimate target of attack. The lethal threat from terrorism, therefore, cannot be separated from our reliance on foreign oil. American leaders are not unaware of this danger. Months before Sept. 11, 2001, President Bush warned of the dangers associated with growing U.S. dependence on imports from the developing world. "If we fail to act," he declared on May 17 of that year, "our country will become more reliant on foreign crude oil, putting our national energy security into the hands of foreign nations, some of whom do not share our interests." The logical response, of course, would have been to take swift action to diminish America's dependence on imports. But this would have required a substantial reduction in our consumption of oil and a dramatic improvement in the fuel efficiency of American automobiles—steps that Bush was clearly unwilling to take, presumably because this would jeopardize the profits of his friends and associates in the petroleum industry. As a result, we are far more dependent on imported oil today than we were in 2001.

America Is Too Reluctant to Conserve Oil

It follows that efforts to substantially reduce America's oil dependency will prove far more difficult in 2005 and the years thereafter than they would have been if we had started down this path in 2001. For example, if we had imposed significant fuel-efficiency requirements for cars and SUVs in 2001, we would now be saving a million or more barrels of oil per day; instead, overall fleet efficiency actually declined over this period, and so we are that much further behind the curve. To catch up with where we might have been had we moved sooner will require far more stringent requirements in the years ahead—and it is this awesome prospect that has deterred the major candidates from raising the oil issue in a meaningful way. They may pay lip service to the perils of dependency, but are unwilling to advocate the decisive steps that are required to make a meaningful difference. Kerry is more outspoken on this issue than Bush—he has proposed a $10 billion fund to promote new automobile technology and other energy innovations—but has not called for mandatory increases in automobile fuel efficiency, the only sure way to reduce net petroleum dependency.

With crude oil fetching a record $50 per barrel and prices rising at the pump, Bush and Kerry are both likely to promise vigorous action to resolve the crisis. Both will also tout their respective solutions to dependency: drilling in ANWR in Bush's case, accelerated development of new technologies in Kerry's. But neither will acknowledge the magnitude of the problem or offer the sort of remedies that can really make a difference. The dependency dilemma will intensify, therefore, and we can expect bigger oil shocks in the years ahead. Environmentalists will, of course, keep pushing for tougher action, but we may have to wait for a truly massive crisis—entailing a global economic meltdown—before our leaders give this issue the attention it deserves.

> *"Every dollar the federal government borrows makes us less secure as a nation, by making America beholden to interests outside our borders."*

The Federal Debt Is a Threat to National Security

Ron Paul

Texas congressman Ron Paul claims in the following viewpoint that America is reaching its borrowing limit with foreign investors and will likely experience serious economic consequences when the debt is recalled. Paul maintains that this dependency on outside money has made the United States a slave of other countries, leaving America vulnerable to the whims of foreign governments. Paul insists that America must work to pay off its debts or jeopardize the security of the nation.

As you read, consider the following questions:

1. According to Paul, since what year has America spent more than it has received in revenues?

Ron Paul, "Government Debt: The Greatest Threat to National Security," October 25, 2004. www.house.gov/paul.

2. Where does the author say that Asian banks and investors are now more likely to invest their money?

3. How could China and other large shareholders in U.S. Treasury bills wage "economic war" against America, in Paul's view?

Once again the federal government has reached its "debt ceiling," and once again Congress is poised to authorize an increase in government borrowing. Between its ever-growing bureaucracies, expanding entitlements, and overseas military entanglements, the federal government is borrowing roughly one billion dollars *every day* to pay its bills.

Federal law limits the amount of debt the U.S. Treasury may carry, and the current amount—a whopping $7.4 *trillion*—has been reached once again by a spendthrift federal government. Total federal spending, which now exceeds $2 trillion annually, once took more than 100 years to double. Today it doubles in less than a decade, and the rate is accelerating. When President [Ronald] Reagan entered office in 1981 facing a federal debt of $1 trillion that had piled up over the decades, he declared that figure "incomprehensible." At its present rate of spending, the federal government will soon amass $1 trillion of new debt in just *one year*.

Blissfully Unaware of the Crisis Ahead

Government debt carries absolutely no stigma for politicians in Washington. The original idea behind the debt limit law was to shine a light on government spending, by forcing lawmakers to vote publicly for debt increases. Over time, however, the increases have become so commonplace that the media scarcely reports them—and there are no political consequences for those who vote for more red ink. It's far more risky for politicians to vote against special-interest spending.

Impact of Budget Cuts on the Army

Pentagon officials are being told by the White House to cut between $13 billion and $15 billion from the 2007 defense budget and trim tens of billions more in coming years. . . .

The Army, which is heavily engaged in combat operations and needs the extra 40,000 troops Congress voted to give them (at a cost of $18 billion), has few programs it can afford to cut. It may have to simply scrap equipment worn out in operations in Iraq and Afghanistan rather than repair it. Yet, to replace this equipment in future years would be much more expensive, while doing without the equipment weakens the fighting power of our forces. This is clearly a "penny wise, pound foolish" approach.

William R. Hawkins, AmericanEconomicAlert.org,
October 31, 2005.

Since 1969, the federal government has spent more than it received in revenues every year. Even supposed single-year surpluses never existed, but were merely an accounting trick based on stealing IOUs from the imaginary Social Security trust fund. Remember that the total federal debt continued to rise rapidly even during the claimed surplus years. Since Congress is incapable of spending only what the Treasury takes in, it must borrow money. Unlike ordinary debts, however, government debts are not repaid by those who spend the money—they're repaid by you and future generations.

The federal government issues U.S. Treasury bonds to finance its deficit spending. The largest holders of those Treasury notes—our largest creditors—are foreign governments and foreign individuals. Asian central banks and investors in particular, especially China, have been happy to buy U.S. dollars over the past decade. But foreign governments will not prop up our spending habits forever. Already, Asian central banks are favoring Euro-denominated assets over U.S. dollars, reflecting their belief that the American economy is headed for trouble. It's akin to a credit-card company cutting off a borrower who has exceeded his credit limit one too many times.

Debt Slavery

Debt destroys U.S. sovereignty, because the American economy now depends on the actions of foreign governments. While we brag about our role as world superpower in international affairs, we are in truth the world's greatest debtor. Like all debtors, we are not truly free. China and other foreign government creditors could in essence wage economic war against us simply by dumping their huge holdings of U.S. dollars, driving the value of those dollars sharply downward and severely damaging our economy. Desmond Lachman, an economist at the American Enterprise Institute, states that foreign central banks "now have considerable ability to disrupt U.S. financial markets by simply deciding to refrain from buying further U.S. government paper." Former Treasury secretary Lawrence Summers warns about "a kind of global balance of financial terror," noting our dependency on "the discretionary acts of what are inevitably political entities in other countries."

Ultimately, debt is slavery. Every dollar the federal government borrows makes us less secure as a nation, by making America beholden to interests outside our borders. So when you hear a politician saying America will do "whatever it takes" to fight terrorism or rebuild Iraq or end poverty or provide health care for all, what they really mean is they are willing to sink America even deeper into debt. We're told that foreign wars and expanded entitlements will somehow make America more secure, but insolvency is hardly the foundation for security. Only when we stop trying to remake the world in our image, and reject the entitlement state at home, will we begin to create a more secure America that is not a financial slave to foreign creditors.

Periodical Bibliography

The following articles have been selected to supplement the diverse views presented in this chapter.

Mike Allen et al.	"The End of Cowboy Diplomacy," *Time*, July 17, 2006.
William M. Arkin	"The Continuing Misuses of Fear," *Bulletin of the Atomic Scientists*, September/October 2006.
Barry Buzan	"Will the 'Global War on Terrorism' Be the New Cold War?" *International Affairs*, November 2006.
David Cortright	"The New Nuclear Danger: A Strategy of Selective Coercion Is Fundamentally Flawed," *America*, December 11, 2006.
Robert Dreyfuss	"The Phony War," *Rolling Stone*, September 21, 2006.
Geoffrey Forden	"How the World's Most Underdeveloped Nations Get the World's Most Dangerous Weapons," *Technology & Culture*, January 2007.
Vinod Khosla	"The War on Oil," *Wall Street Journal*, January 23, 2007.
Mark Mazzetti	"Spy Agencies Say Iraq War Worsens Terrorism Threat," *New York Times*, September 24, 2006.
National Review	"The Biggest Threat We Face," August 28, 2006.
Susan E. Rice	"The Threat of Global Poverty," *National Interest*, Spring 2006.
Bradley A. Thayer	"In Defense of Primacy," *National Interest*, November/December 2006.
Evan Thomas et al.	"The New Age of Terror," *Newsweek*, August 28, 2006.

OPPOSING
VIEWPOINTS®
SERIES

CHAPTER 2

How Should the U. S. Deal with Nations That Threaten National Security?

Chapter Preface

On January 29, 2002, President George W. Bush delivered his State of the Union address in the aftermath of the September 11, 2001, terrorist attacks in New York and Washington, D.C. Recognizing that U.S. national security had been so easily breached by a handful of radical operatives, the president warned the country that it would have to protect itself by taking on rogue nations and terrorist organizations before they could inflict more grievous damage against the free world.

As one of the stated goals in his speech, Bush asserted that America would need to prevent nations such as North Korea and Iran from building or acquiring weapons of mass destruction (WMD) and stop the murderous regime in Iraq which, he said, had already used chemical weapons on its own people and was attempting to further its bid for a nuclear arsenal. President Bush declared, "States like these, and their terrorist allies, constitute an axis of evil, arming to threaten the peace of the world. By seeking weapons of mass destruction, these regimes pose a grave and growing danger. They could provide these arms to terrorists, giving them the means to match their hatred. They could attack our allies or attempt to blackmail the United States. In any of these cases, the price of indifference would be catastrophic."

Just over a year later, the Bush administration ordered the invasion of Iraq to topple the rule of Saddam Hussein and supposedly destroy his stockpiles of chemical weapons as well as facilities that allegedly were developing nuclear materials. After a short, decisive ground war, Saddam's regime fell, but even after months of searching, U.S. forces could not find any weapons of mass destruction. The administration contended, however, that the war had freed oppressed Iraqis, stopped any pursuit of WMD, and severed connections between Saddam and Islamic terrorists. Four years after the invasion, America still has a large troop presence in Iraq to keep order in a land that is close to civil war.

Perhaps because it has tied up its ground forces in Iraq, the United States has yet to follow a similar military strategy in either Iran or North Korea. Just prior to the invasion of Iraq, North Korea withdrew from the Nuclear Nonproliferation Treaty because it supposedly felt threatened by America's hostile posture. Officials in Pyongyang stated their desire to build nuclear weapons as a deterrent to American aggressiveness, and on October 9, 2006, the North Koreans tested a weapon that supposedly had a nuclear payload. Similarly, Iran began uranium enrichment programs in the early twenty-first century and announced in April 2006 that it had successfully accomplished that task. The European Union and the United Nations have tried to offer Iran economic assistance packages to entice it to stop its enrichment program—which could lead to the development of nuclear weapons—but Iran has snubbed each offer. The United States has pushed for talks with both Iran and North Korea, making some headway with the latter when, in February 2007, the North Koreans agreed to shut down the nation's nuclear reactor. However, America has always kept military strikes as a viable alternative should negotiations fail.

In the following chapter, U.S. policy analysts comment on the course of action the United States should pursue with each of the nations in President Bush's axis of evil. In each case, the commentators strive to balance national security interests against the potential of exacerbating a crisis that could have global consequences.

> "We fight today because terrorists want to attack our country and kill our citizens, and Iraq is where they are making their stand."

The United States Must Stay in Iraq

George W. Bush

George W. Bush is the forty-third president of the United States. In the following viewpoint, Bush claims that the United States will stay committed to its present involvement in Iraq because Iraq is a major battlefield in the war on terrorism.

According to Bush, withdrawing U.S. troops from Iraq would give terrorists and other anti-American forces a victory that would come back to haunt America. In his view, a fallen Iraq would become a safe harbor from which terrorists could launch more attacks against the United States or its allies.

As you read, consider the following questions:

1. What is the U.S mission in Iraq, according to Bush?
2. As the author states, which other nations are the resistance forces in Iraq coming from?

George W. Bush, "President Addresses Nation, Discusses Iraq, War on Terror," June 28, 2005. www.whitehouse.gov.

3. What, in Bush's view, are the only ways in which the terrorists can succeed against the advance of freedom?

The troops here and across the world are fighting a global war on terror. The war reached our shores on September the 11th, 2001. The terrorists who attacked us—and the terrorists we face—murder in the name of a totalitarian ideology that hates freedom, rejects tolerance, and despises all dissent. Their aim is to remake the Middle East in their own grim image of tyranny and oppression by toppling governments, by driving us out of the region, and by exporting terror.

To achieve these aims, they have continued to kill in Madrid, Istanbul, Jakarta, Casablanca, Riyadh, Bali, and elsewhere. The terrorists believe that free societies are essentially corrupt and decadent and with a few hard blows, they can force us to retreat. They are mistaken. After September the 11th, I made a commitment to the American people: This Nation will not wait to be attacked again. We will defend our freedom. We will take the fight to the enemy.

Iraq Is a Battlefield in the War on Terror

Iraq is the latest battlefield in this war. Many terrorists who kill innocent men, women, and children on the streets of Baghdad [in Iraq] are followers of the same murderous ideology that took the lives of our citizens in New York, in Washington, and Pennsylvania [on September 11, 2001]. There is only one course of action against them, to defeat them abroad before they attack us at home. The commander in charge of coalition operations in Iraq, who is also senior commander at this base, General John Vines, put it well the other day. He said, "We either deal with terrorism and this extremism abroad, or we deal with it when it comes to us."

Our mission in Iraq is clear. We're hunting down the terrorists. We're helping Iraqis build a free nation that is an ally in the war on terror. We're advancing freedom in the broader

A Feasible Victory in Iraq

Rather than attempting to micromanage Iraqi politics and engineer the government and constitution, the United States should concentrate on destroying the international terrorists who have flocked to Iraq and preventing them from turning the country into a base. . . .

The United States can achieve a realistic victory in Iraq without killing every last insurgent, capturing every Al-Qaeda recruit, ironing out every dispute between Arabs and Kurds, Sunnis and Shi'as, secularists and Islamists, or solving every other thorny political or constitutional problem. Americans and others will recognize victory if we have managed to break the back of less than 10% of original Al-Qaeda in Iraq and left in place an Iraqi government committed and able to prevent the jihadists from returning. Then the United States can turn its attention to other pressing problems that threaten the peace and prosperity of the Republic.

Nikolas K. Gvosdev, National Interest, *Fall 2005.*

Middle East. We are removing a source of violence and instability and laying the foundation of peace for our children and our grandchildren.

The work in Iraq is difficult, and it is dangerous. Like most Americans, I see the images of violence and bloodshed. Every picture is horrifying, and the suffering is real. Amid all this violence, I know Americans ask the question: Is the sacrifice worth it? It is worth it, and it is vital to the future security of our country. And tonight I will explain the reasons why.

The Terrorists' Intentions

Some of the violence you see in Iraq is being carried out by ruthless killers who are converging on Iraq to fight the ad-

vance of peace and freedom. Our military reports that we've
killed or captured hundreds of foreign fighters in Iraq who
have come from Saudi Arabia and Syria, Iran, Egypt, Sudan,
Yemen, Libya, and others. They are making common cause
with criminal elements, Iraqi insurgents, and remnants of
Saddam Hussein's regime who want to restore the old order.
They fight because they know that the survival of their hateful
ideology is at stake. They know that as freedom takes root in
Iraq, it will inspire millions across the Middle East to claim
their liberty as well. And when the Middle East grows in democracy and prosperity and hope, the terrorists will lose their
sponsors, lose their recruits, and lose their hopes for turning
that region into a base for attacks on America and our allies
around the world.

Some wonder whether Iraq is a central front in the war on
terror. Among the terrorists, there is no debate. Hear the
words of Usama bin Laden: "This third world war is raging"
in Iraq. "The whole world is watching this war." He says it will
end in "victory and glory, or misery and humiliation."

The terrorists know that the outcome will leave them em-
boldened or defeated. So they are waging a campaign of murder and destruction. And there is no limit to the innocent
lives they are willing to take.

We see the nature of the enemy in terrorists who exploded
car bombs along a busy shopping street in Baghdad, including
one outside a mosque. We see the nature of the enemy in terrorists who sent a suicide bomber to a teaching hospital in
Mosul. We see the nature of the enemy in terrorists who be-
head civilian hostages and broadcast their atrocities for the
world to see.

Terror Cannot Prevail

These are savage acts of violence, but they have not brought
the terrorists any closer to achieving their strategic objectives.
The terrorists, both foreign and Iraqi, failed to stop the trans-

fer of sovereignty. They failed to break our coalition and force a mass withdrawal by our allies. They failed to incite an Iraqi civil war. They failed to prevent free elections. They failed to stop the formation of a democratic Iraqi Government that represents all of Iraq's diverse population. And they failed to stop Iraqis from signing up in large number with the police forces and the army to defend their new democracy.

The lesson of this experience is clear: The terrorists can kill the innocent, but they cannot stop the advance of freedom. The only way our enemies can succeed is if we forget the lessons of September the 11th, if we abandon the Iraqi people to men like [al Qaeda terrorist leader in Iraq, Abu Musab al-] Zarqawi, and if we yield the future of the Middle East to men like bin Laden. For the sake of our Nation's security, this will not happen on my watch. . . .

America Makes a Stand

America and our friends are in a conflict that demands much of us. It demands the courage of our fighting men and women. It demands the steadfastness of our allies, and it demands the perseverance of our citizens. We accept these burdens, because we know what is at stake. We fight today because Iraq now carries the hope of freedom in a vital region of the world, and the rise of democracy will be the ultimate triumph over radicalism and terror. And we fight today because terrorists want to attack our country and kill our citizens, and Iraq is where they are making their stand. So we'll fight them there. We'll fight them across the world, and we will stay in the fight until the fight is won.

America has done difficult work before. From our desperate fight for independence to the darkest days of a Civil War to the hard-fought battles against tyranny in the 20th century, there were many chances to lose our heart, our nerve, or our way. But Americans have always held firm, because we have always believed in certain truths. We know that if evil is not confronted, it gains in strength and audacity and returns to strike us again. We know that when the work is hard, the proper response is not retreat; it is courage. And we know that this great ideal of human freedom is entrusted to us in a special way and that the ideal of liberty is worth defending.

| "*Being bogged down in Iraq hampers our ability to deal with threats in Iran and Afghanistan.*"

The United States Must Leave Iraq

Brian Katulis

In the following viewpoint, Brian Katulis contends that U.S. forces should be redeployed from Iraq and power should be handed over to the new Iraqi government. Katulis maintains that the United States cannot station its military indefinitely in Iraq because of the soaring costs of upkeep and the fact that the military may be needed to address national security interests elsewhere. Brian Katulis is the director of democracy and public diplomacy at the Center for American Progress, a progressive think tank.

As you read, consider the following questions:

1. As Katulis relates, what did a Pentagon-commissioned study conclude about the military consequences of the current pace of operations in Iraq?

Brian Katulis, "Changing Direction in Iraq: The Case for Redeployment," Center for American Progress, June 20, 2006. This material was created by the Center for American Progress, www.americanprogress.org. Reproduced by permission.

2. What does the author hope a newly appointed envoy to Iraq might accomplish in a much-needed U.S. peace conference concerning Iraq?

3. What are the goals of Katulis's proposed shift in strategic policy that would focus on stabilizing Iraq and the gulf region?

[The June 7, 2006] killing of terrorist [and al Qaeda leader] Abu Musab al-Zarqawi was a major success for our troops in Iraq. But Zarqawi's elimination is unlikely to stabilize Iraq, as violence and lawlessness continue to plague many parts of the country.

To take advantage of the momentum achieved by getting rid of Zarqawi, the [George W.] Bush administration should take concrete steps to put the Iraqis in control of their own affairs. President Bush's deliberations at Camp David [in mid-2006] should result in a clear signal that the time for U.S. troops to start coming home is near.

One of the best incentives that the United States can use to motivate Iraq's new government is to put them on notice and set target dates for completing the U.S. military mission. The only time Iraq has seen progress [since the U.S. invasion in 2003] is when the United States set out clear deadlines for the political transition process.

The time has come for the United States to redeploy its troops and intensify its political and diplomatic efforts to help Iraq's leaders strike the power-sharing deals needed to stabilize their country.

Bogged Down in Iraq

The Bush administration's many mistakes in Iraq—invading for the wrong reasons and without enough troops, as well as not having a clear strategy for Iraq's political transition and reconstruction—have undermined U.S. power and its reputation. The United States cannot practically pull out its troops

Quelling Resistance by Leaving Iraq

Those who favor a quick exit point out that withdrawing will actually go a long way toward satisfying the demands of the warring factions in Iraq. The Sunni population that provided the base of Saddam's support—including the current leaders of the Iraqi resistance—would be more likely to participate in the political process if the United States pulls out, providing a counterbalance to the theocratic and paramilitary Shiite parties who currently control Iraq's fledgling government. That, in turn, would reduce Iran's influence in Baghdad, where the Iranian-backed Badr Corps is keeping the Supreme Council for Islamic Revolution in power. And once the U.S. occupation ends, most analysts believe, the ability of Al Qaeda to attract recruits will largely evaporate, since it is the anger over the presence of American troops in Iraq that provides Al Qaeda with its best sales pitch. . . .

In fact, the main force of the Iraqi resistance fighting the United States is drawn not from Al Qaeda but from the former Iraqi army and Republican Guard, which dissolved after the war. Many insurgents are also what Iraq experts call POIs, or "pissed-off Iraqis"—mostly Sunni Arabs who hate the idea that Iraq is occupied by U.S. troops.

Robert Dreyfuss, Rolling Stone, *November 17, 2005.*

tomorrow—and leaving precipitously risks an all-out civil war that could spill over Iraq's borders.

But the United States cannot keep its troops in Iraq indefinitely. The costs of the current course are unsustainable—nearly 2,500 U.S. military personnel killed and 18,000 wounded, more than $300 billion spent, and U.S. ground forces stretched to the breaking point. The extended deployments in Iraq have eroded U.S. ground forces and overall military strength. A Pentagon-commissioned study concluded that the Army cannot maintain its current pace of operations in Iraq without doing permanent damage to the quality of the force. Also, being bogged down in Iraq hampers our ability to deal with threats in Iran and Afghanistan.

The key question now is: What should the United States do to minimize the risks of the eventual withdrawal of U.S. troops?

Withdrawal Strategy

Expectations must change to fit today's grim realities. The administration must recognize that Iraq is not yet a real democracy, nor will it be anytime soon, and a new government in Iraq is not going to trigger a wave of democracy in the Middle East. Americans need and deserve a clear exit strategy for Iraq that spells out how much longer U.S. troops will be involved and what it will cost. Iraq's leaders need to understand that the United States is not going to serve as a crutch indefinitely.

In a report released [in fall 2005] and updated [in] spring [2006], [Center for American Progress Fellow] Lawrence Korb and I made the case for a responsible exit strategy in Iraq called "Strategic Redeployment." This five-part strategy addresses the challenges the United States faces in Iraq, Afghanistan, and the broader threat by terrorist networks and extreme regimes.

The United States should announce that it will not maintain permanent bases in Iraq and that it will withdraw all its forces by the end of 2007, by gradually reducing its troop presence in Iraq to 60,000 by the end of 2006, and to zero by the end of 2007.

Troops remaining in Iraq through 2007 would train Iraqi forces, eradicate terrorist cells, provide logistical support to Iraqi forces, and provide border security. The United States should also leave an Army division in Kuwait, place a Marine expeditionary force and a carrier battle group in the Persian Gulf, and double the number of troops in Afghanistan.

Restructuring a Divided Nation

The United States must recognize that Iraq has become a failed state with major internal problems, and it should take appropriate diplomatic action to bring peace and stability to Iraq. President Bush should appoint an envoy, with the stature of a former secretary of state, to organize a Geneva peace conference under UN auspices. The conference would aim to broker a deal on the division of power, security, militias, and the allocation of oil resources.

The Bush administration should launch a Gulf Stability Initiative, a multilateral diplomatic effort to develop a regional security framework for confidence-building measures and regional security cooperation among countries in the region. This framework would be helpful in dealing also with the growing nuclear capabilities of Iran.

The Bush administration should correct the mistakes it made to date in its reconstruction efforts by supporting international funds to provide emergency humanitarian and economic assistance. These development projects should give priority to hiring Iraqis.

The United States should develop a more realistic strategy to confront falsehoods promoted by its extremist adversaries. The United States should make key policy shifts—including trying to stabilize the situation between Israelis and Palestinians.

The end goals of this strategic shift are clear: to protect the American people at home and abroad; to get Iraq to the most stable position as quickly as possible; to make sure Iraq's tensions do not spill over into a regional conflict; and to turn the tide against extremist Islamists who continue to threaten the United States nearly five years after the Sept. 11 attacks.

The time has come for the United States to change direction in Iraq. The United States should complete its military mission in Iraq at a time of our choosing. The time has come to set target dates to redeploy U.S. troops. Not setting a target date leaves U.S. national security hostage to events. Americans in the end will be safer if our Army is rested and ready to take on necessary assignments, if our National Guard is home to respond to terrorist attacks and other disasters, and if terrorists can no longer use Iraq as a recruiting tool. The time has come for decisive action to put the United States back in charge of its own national security. Strategic redeployment will accomplish that goal.

> *"Iran's nuclear advance is a dramatic escalation in an already tense regional cold war. And that, for all strategic purposes, is an act of aggression."*

The United States Should Consider Military Action Against Iran

Mario Loyola

A former consultant to the Department of Defense, Mario Loyola is a visiting fellow at the Foundation for the Defense of Democracies. In the following viewpoint, he warns that if Iran continues to pursue its nuclear agenda, then the United States will have to take action. Loyola states that Washington will try to pressure the Iranian government to give up its ambitions. Failing that, however, the United States must be prepared for military action because, in Loyola's view, Iran's gambit in pursuing nuclear weapons must be considered an act of aggression.

As you read, consider the following questions:

1. As Loyola enumerates, what would be the targets of a "cradle-to-grave" strike bent on curtailing Iranian nuclear weapons development?

Mario Loyola, "Can Their Program Be Destroyed? The Military Options against the Mullahs," *National Review*, vol. 58, no. 19, October 23, 2006, pp. 36–38. Copyright © 2006 by National Review, Inc., 215 Lexington Avenue, New York, NY 10016. Reproduced by permission.

2. What advantages does the author say the United States would have in a war against Iran?

3. In Loyola's view, what is the first and most important line of defense in the age of weapons of mass destruction?

At Natanz, about 130 miles from Tehran [Iran's capital] the Iranian regime is constructing a vast "commercial scale" uranium-enrichment facility that will house as many as 55,000 centrifuges. Deep under several meters of steel-reinforced concrete, conveniently out of reach of the most powerful known conventional bunker-busters, the facility will be able to produce sizeable quantities of lightly enriched uranium (LEU) in a matter of months once it is operational. The steps required to enrich LEU all the way to highly enriched, weapons-grade uranium are few and have been described by experts as purely mechanical.

Some have argued that operational launch of these main "enrichment cascades" at Natanz . . . should in and of itself be considered a red line by U.S. officials—i.e., a line Iran must not be permitted to cross. But Iran is generally cooperating with inspectors from the International Atomic Energy Agency [IAEA]: If it continues to do so, and if the plant's operations remain transparent, the [George W.] Bush administration is likely to conclude that it can hold its breath for a little while to see how things develop. It will be a nail-biting period of months; intelligence assessments will be studied nervously; allies will be consulted weekly; and the most minor IAEA inspections will be followed minutely.

Iran will be on notice—but the prize within the mullahs' reach may be just too tantalizing. In a 2004 article in *Asia Times*, Kaveh Afrasiabi, a Tehran University political-science professor who is close to former high-ranking officials in the regime, put Tehran's thinking starkly:

There is an emerging "proto-nuclear deterrence" according to which Iran's mastery of the nuclear fuel cycle would make it "nuclear weapon capable" in a relatively short time, as a sort of pre-weapon "threshold capability" that must be taken into account by Iran's enemies contemplating attacks on its nuclear installations. Such attacks would be met by stiff resistance, born of Iran's historic sense of nationalism and patriotism, as well as by a counter-weaponization based on quick conversion of the nuclear technology. Hence, the longer the U.S., and Israel, keep up the military threat, the more powerful and appealing the Iranian yearning for a "proto-nuclear deterrence" will grow.

This window into the regime's thinking suggests what might happen next. If for some reason—say, a sudden increase in Mideast tensions—Iran stops cooperating with the IAEA, we will suddenly find ourselves at a point of no return. We will no longer be able to know what Iran is doing with its nuclear capabilities. The crisis will finally arrive for decision in the Oval Office, just as it did—albeit in much simpler form—for the [Bill] Clinton administration, in the North Korean nuclear crisis of 1994 [in which Clinton contemplated bombing North Korea's nuclear facilities but ultimately acceded to a negotiated settlement]. . . .

Military Strike Options

An Iranian decision to stop cooperating with the IAEA will trigger a similar crisis in the U.S. national-security establishment. The options are likely to be presented from "lightest" to "heaviest," according to a progression calibrated to anticipate Tehran's likely reaction to any military strike. The "lightest" option could consist of limited strikes on the handful of facilities directly related to uranium enrichment. The most important of these are buried deep underground at Natanz. Experts believe we could not be confident of completely destroying the facilities if we relied only on conventional air strikes, even if we resorted to repeated strikes on the same targets in the hope of creating craters within craters deep enough to reach the facilities.

Unfortunately, the alternatives to conventional air strikes are few, and they tend to the outlandish. Nuclear bunker-busters are certainly out of the question, if indeed they exist at all. Other possibilities are helicopter-borne missions using special-operations forces, and a "thunder run": a swift, heavily armed ground incursion by large-unit forces operating out of Iraq or Afghanistan.

But given the degree of skepticism attaching to the likely success of "light strikes" in setting back Iran's nuclear program, the Joint Chiefs are likely to recommend that any strikes seek to destroy Iran's nuclear program "cradle-to-grave": from uranium mining, to conversion facilities, to enrichment facilities, to hard-water plants, to the various reactors now under construction. A crucial element in these strikes would be Iran's nuclear know-how. This would mean that, for the first time in history, the offices and laboratories of university faculty may become military targets. Such a "strike package" might set Iran's nuclear program back ten years, although many experts are more pessimistic.

Because Iran's nuclear facilities are so dispersed and, in many cases, well defended, estimates of the number of possible targets for this option range from 300 to 1,500. Given these numbers, the mission could not be accomplished exclusively with stealth aircraft. Hundreds of relatively slow-moving non-stealth aircraft would be involved—so the initial phases of the operation would have to wipe out Iran's national air defenses. That in turn would mean an operation lasting many days or even weeks.

Iranian Retaliation

When the smoke settles, Tehran will not delay in retaliating somehow. It is likely to perceive that its room for maneuver is somewhat constrained, because while everyone knows that the U.S. is reluctant to invade Iran, an Iranian retaliation could be so serious as to force the U.S. into an all-out war. And yet there are many possible acts of retaliation Iran could commit before triggering an all-out U.S. invasion. Iran possesses a significant arsenal of long- and medium-range missiles, and could use them against countries that facilitate any U.S. action—or against Israel, as Iran has already threatened.

Iran's most fearsome counter-deterrent to the destruction of its nuclear facilities is the implied threat to ruin America's project in Iraq. But here, the U.S. has a deep strategic advantage. The success of democracy in Iraq is rapidly becoming not America's fight, but rather that of Iraq's Shiite majority—the very group that Tehran seeks most avidly and actively to protect. One of Iraq's most important Shiite political parties—the Supreme Council for the Islamic Revolution in Iraq—is a key player in the government, and it was created in Iran to fight Saddam [Hussein]. Thus, in order to ruin the U.S. effort in Iraq, Iran must first directly and vividly ruin the project of the very factions that are friendliest to it.

It is worth remembering, also, that a huge military force is parked on Iran's western and eastern borders. One might think that this force is largely tied down in Iraq now, but . . . it has slowly withdrawn from large-scale forward operations. In a sense, Iran's nuclear program may now be in a race against time, while America's assets and options multiply.

Furthermore, Iran's military is surprisingly weak. Its army has on the order of 300,000 troops, covering a country four times the size of Iraq. It would never be able to stop the advance of a single American mechanized or armored brigade on a "thunder run." The country is, tactically speaking, essentially wide open for military operations of many kinds. It was perhaps because of this that, reportedly, some of Iran's most senior generals recently wrote a letter to [Iran's supreme leader] Ayatollah Ali Khamenei warning that [Iranian president Mahmoud] Ahmadinejad was embarking on a dangerous course of action, and that Iran could not risk war with the U.S.

Beyond military retaliation, Iran might launch a worldwide terror campaign against America. The regime claims that the Revolutionary Guards have established a "Lovers of Martyrdom Garrison" of suicide bombers for this very purpose, with thousands of recruits. But, as some experts have pointed out, one thing the current War on Terror has not seen is the phenomenon of Shiite—much less Persian—suicide bombers. Thankfully, the suicide-bombing tactic is thus far almost exclusively the domain of Sunni Arabs. With a view to the looming confrontation, Iran is also preparing to shut down the Strait of Hormuz, through which passes 40 percent of the world's oil. But the Tehran regime derives 65 percent of its revenue from oil shipments, almost all of which must pass through the Strait of Hormuz—making this, too, an unattractive option.

Facing an Act of Aggression

Taking into account Tehran's options for retaliation after any initial strike, heavier strike packages would target known missile forces, the air force, the Revolutionary Guards and other military bases, command and control, and naval assets along the Persian Gulf. The U.S. may devise its plan "backwards," from the desired result to a specific military strategy. That's what the U.S. did in [the Serbian province of] Kosovo. The air campaign designed by Gen. Wesley Clark struck first at the [Slobodan] Milosevic regime's most essential command-and-control assets. After initial operations to degrade Serbia's air defense, NATO [North Atlantic Treaty Organization] passed immediately to the core facilities of the Defense Ministry, paralyzing the regime's military capability from the inside out. And then NATO started to remove the regime's ability to function as a state, destroying key transportation infrastruc-

ture, energy resources, and communications facilities. It did all that, and even put a cruise missile in Milosevic's bedroom, before shifting its focus to the ultimate objective: the Serbian ground forces in Kosovo.

That's what Iran will likely face. The Iranian regime has to be made to understand that in the current state of Middle East confrontation, in which many Americans have already been killed because of Iranian-inspired acts of aggression, their acquisition of a nuclear breakout capability represents a grave threat to the U.S.—and a potentially fatal threat to Israel—and that the West is grimly aware of this. Iran's nuclear advance is a dramatic escalation in an already tense regional cold war. And that, for all strategic purposes, is an act of aggression.

International law has never devised an authoritative definition of aggression. But, strategically speaking, the definition is quite clear: Any act that directly threatens the security of other states is an act of aggression. As [former United Nations secretary-general] Kofi Annan said to the General Assembly some years ago, "It is not enough to denounce unilateralism unless we also face up squarely to the concerns that make some states feel uniquely vulnerable, since it is those concerns that drive them to take unilateral action."

Iran Has Not Negotiated in Good Faith

Irredentist powers often seek to alter the status quo in order to advance important aims. They must then typically choose between a laborious process of negotiation aimed at leaving all parties satisfied, or achieving the alteration quickly and aggressively. China, for example, has shown an increased willingness to choose the path of negotiating in good faith, even if that means deferring strategic goals that may already be within its reach unilaterally; its bid to exploit mineral claims in the South China Sea comes immediately to mind.

Iran has at times suggested that it might be willing to do this, but in fact the West's negotiations with Iran have not slowed down the regime's multi-track nuclear advance. Iran's goal in the negotiations is to provide assurances to the Europeans, regardless of whether the U.S. also accepts them—in a bid to divide the international community. Iran, in short, is not negotiating in good faith.

To insist that Iran be transparently peaceful in its nuclear activities is to insist upon the protection of the greatest benefit of the nonproliferation regime: transparency. That is the first and most important line of defense in the age of WMD [weapons of mass destruction]. Especially in the case of hostile terror-sponsors, nuclear nonproliferation is an indispensable element of our national security. If Iran eliminates the hope of maintaining transparent nonproliferation through diplomatic means, it will force upon the United States a choice between abandoning one of the most valuable ramparts of our security—or defending it by force.

Weighing the risks and benefits of a military confrontation with Iran against the risks and benefits of avoiding one will be excruciatingly difficult. The U.S. should push that decision squarely on Iran. Iran is now the power seeking to challenge the status quo—so logically the risk calculation is in the first instance Iran's to make. The object of U.S. policy must be to increase the risks of confrontation such that they become prohibitive to Iran. And the only way to accomplish that is to send a clear message to the Iranian regime that we will not allow it to compromise our national security and push the world farther down the slippery slope of uncontrolled nuclear proliferation.

> "An attack on Iran would be an act of
> political folly, setting in motion a pro-
> gressive upheaval in world affairs."

The United States Should Not Consider Military Action Against Iran

Zbigniew Brzezinski

In the following viewpoint, Zbigniew Brzezinski advises against pursuing military action to stop Iran from obtaining nuclear weapons. Brzezinski states that military strikes would only stir up more Middle Eastern hatred against America and would likely involve the United States in a war that it could not win. Brzezinski suggests that initiating serious negotiations with Iran is the best path the United States can take to resolve the nuclear crisis. Zbigniew Brzezinski was national security adviser to President Jimmy Carter.

As you read, consider the following questions:

1. According to Brzezinski, what specific impacts would a U.S. attack on Iran have on other problem areas in the Middle East?

Zbigniew Brzezinski, "Do Not Attack Iran," *International Herald Tribune*, April 26, 2006. Copyright © 2006 by The New York Times Company. Reprinted with permission.

2. Why would it be unlikely, in the author's view, for Iran to hand any nuclear weapons over to terrorists?

3. Why does Brzezinski believe that the mullahs are Iran's past?

Iran's announcement [in mid-2006] that it has enriched a minute amount of uranium has unleashed urgent calls for a preventive U.S. air strike by the same sources that earlier urged war on Iraq.

If there is another terrorist attack in the United States, you can bet your bottom dollar that there will be also immediate charges that Iran was responsible in order to generate public hysteria in favor of military action.

Reasons to Avoid Military Strikes

But there are four compelling reasons against a preventive air attack on Iranian nuclear facilities:

1. In the absence of an imminent threat (with the Iranians at least several years away from having a nuclear arsenal), the attack would be a unilateral act of war.

If undertaken without formal Congressional declaration, it would be unconstitutional and merit the impeachment of the president. Similarly, if undertaken without the sanction of the UN Security Council either alone by the United States or in complicity with Israel, it would stamp the perpetrator(s) as an international outlaw(s).

2. Likely Iranian reactions would significantly compound ongoing U.S. difficulties in Iraq and in Afghanistan, perhaps precipitate new violence by [the Lebanese terrorist group] Hezbollah in Lebanon, and in all probability cause the United States to become bogged down in regional violence for a decade or more to come. Iran is a country of some 70 million people and a conflict with it would make the misadventure in Iraq look trivial.

3. Oil prices would climb steeply, especially if the Iranians cut their production and seek to disrupt the flow of oil from

the nearby Saudi oil fields. The world economy would be severely impacted, with America blamed for it. Note that oil prices have already shot above $70 per barrel, in part because of fears of a U.S./Iran clash.

4. America would become an even more likely target of terrorism, with much of the world concluding that America's support for Israel is itself a major cause of the rise in terrorism. America would become more isolated and thus more vulnerable while prospects for an eventual regional accommodation between Israel and its neighbors would be ever more remote.

The End of American Influence

It follows that an attack on Iran would be an act of political folly, setting in motion a progressive upheaval in world affairs. With America increasingly the object of widespread hostility, the era of American preponderance could come to a premature end.

While America is clearly preponderant in the world, it does not have the power—nor the domestic inclination—to both impose and then to sustain its will in the face of protracted and costly resistance. That certainly is the lesson taught both by its Vietnamese and Iraqi experiences.

Moreover, persistent hints by official spokesmen that "the military option is on the table" impedes the kind of negotiations that could make that option redundant. Such threats unite Iranian nationalism with Shiite fundamentalism. They also reinforce growing international suspicions that the United States is even deliberately encouraging greater Iranian intransigence.

Sadly, one has to wonder whether in fact such suspicions may not be partially justified. How else to explain the current U.S. "negotiating" stance: the United States is refusing to participate in the on-going negotiations with Iran but insists on dealing only through proxies. That stands in sharp contrast with the simultaneous negotiations with North Korea [which also has a declared nuclear agenda], in which the United States is actively engaged.

At the same time, the United States is allocating funds for the destabilization of the Iranian regime and is reportedly injecting Special Forces teams into Iran to stir up non-Iranian ethnic minorities in order to fragment the Iranian state (in the name of democratization!). And there are people in the [George W.] Bush administration who do not wish any negotiated solution, abetted by outside drum-beaters for military action and egged on by full-page ads hyping the Iranian threat.

Time for Negotiation

There is unintended but potentially tragic irony in a situation in which the obscene language of President Mahmoud Ahmadinejad (whose powers are actually much more limited than his title implies) helps to justify threats by administration figures who like to hint of mushroom clouds, which in turn help Ahmadinejad to exploit his intransigence to gain more fervent domestic support for himself as well as for the Iranian nuclear program.

It is therefore time for the administration to sober up, to think strategically, with a historic perspective and with America's national interest primarily in mind. Deterrence has worked in U.S.-Soviet relations, in U.S.-Chinese relations, and in Indo-Pakistani relations.

The notion that Iran would someday just hand over the bomb to some terrorist conveniently ignores the fact that doing so would be tantamount to suicide for all of Iran since Iran would be a prime suspect and nuclear forensics would make it difficult to disguise the point of origin.

It is true, however, that an eventual Iranian acquisition of nuclear weapons would heighten tensions in the region. Israel, despite its large nuclear arsenal, would feel less secure. Preventing Iranian acquisition of nuclear weapons is, therefore,

When Might Iran Develop Nuclear Weapons?

While almost no one disputes Iran's nuclear ambitions, there is intense debate over how soon it could get the bomb, and what to do about that. Robert Gallucci, a former government expert on nonproliferation who is now the dean of the School of Foreign Service at Georgetown University, told me [in April 2006], "Based on what I know, Iran could be eight to ten years away" from developing a deliverable nuclear weapon. Gallucci added, "If they had a covert nuclear program and we could prove it, and we could not stop it by negotiation, diplomacy, or the threat of sanctions, I'd be in favor of taking it out. But if you do it"—bomb Iran—"without being able to show there's a secret program, you're in trouble."

Meir Dagan, the head of Mossad, Israel's intelligence agency, told the Knesset [the Israeli parliament in] December [2005] that "Iran is one to two years away, at the latest, from having enriched uranium. From that point, the completion of their nuclear weapon is simply a technical matter." In a conversation with me, a senior Israeli intelligence official talked about what he said was Iran's duplicity: "There are two parallel nuclear programs" inside Iran—the program declared to the I.A.E.A. [International Atomic Energy Agency] and a separate operation, run by the military and the Revolutionary Guards [Iranian elite troops]. Israeli officials have repeatedly made this argument, but Israel has not produced public evidence to support it. Richard Armitage, the Deputy Secretary of State in [George W.] Bush's first term, told me, "I think Iran has a secret nuclear-weapons program—I believe it, but I don't know it."

Seymour M. Hersh, New Yorker, *April 17, 2006.*

justified, but in seeking that goal the United States must bear in mind longer-run prospects for Iran's political and social development.

Iran has the objective preconditions in terms of education, place of women in social affairs and in social aspirations (especially of the youth) to emulate in the foreseeable future the evolution of Turkey. The mullahs [religious leaders] are Iran's past, not its future; it is not in our interest to engage in acts that help to reverse that sequence.

Serious negotiations require not only a patient engagement but also a constructive atmosphere. Artificial deadlines, propounded most often by those who do not wish the United States to negotiate in earnest, are counterproductive. Name-calling and saber-rattling, as well as refusal to even consider the other side's security concerns, can be useful tactics only if the goal is actually to derail the negotiating process.

Dispel the Sense of Urgency

Several conclusions relevant to current U.S. policy stem from the foregoing:

The United States should become a direct participant in the negotiations, joining the three European negotiating states, as well as perhaps Russia and China (both veto-casting UN Security Council members), in direct negotiations with Iran, on the model of the concurrent multilateral talks with North Korea;

As in the case of North Korea, the United States should also simultaneously engage in bilateral talks with Iran regarding mutually contentious security and financial issues;

The United States should be a signatory party to any quid-pro-quo arrangements in the event of a satisfactory resolution of the Iranian nuclear program and of regional security issues.

At some point in the future, the above could perhaps lead to a regional agreement for a nuclear weapons-free zone in the Middle East, especially after the conclusion of an Israeli-

Palestinian peace agreement, endorsed also by all the Arab states of the region. At this stage, however, it would be premature to inject that complicated issue into the negotiating process with Iran.

The choice is either to be stampeded into a reckless adventure profoundly damaging to long-term U.S. national interests or to become serious about giving negotiations with Iran a genuine chance to be productive. The mullahs were on the skids several years ago but were given a new burst of life by the intensifying confrontation with the United States.

The U.S. strategic goal, pursued by real negotiations and not by posturing, should be to separate Iranian nationalism from religious fundamentalism. Treating Iran with respect and within a historical perspective would help to advance that objective.

American policy should not be swayed by a contrived atmosphere of urgency ominously reminiscent of what preceded the intervention in Iraq.

"If the North Koreans launch a threatening [intercontinental ballistic mis-
sile], the president should act in defense of the country and shoot it down."

The United States
Should Employ a Missile
Defense Against North Korea's
Nuclear Weapons

Baker Spring

*Baker Spring is a research fellow in national security policy at
the Heritage Foundation, a conservative think tank. In the following viewpoint, he argues that the United States should utilize
its missile defense system to eliminate any rocket launched toward America or its allies. Spring believes the current defense
system is relatively weak but should be employed nonetheless.
Furthermore, to bolster U.S. defense, he encourages the introduc-
tion of a stronger missile defense plan, such as the Global Protection Against Limited Strikes (GPALS) system that was abandoned in 1991. Spring contends that the current North Korean
threat warrants a reconsideration of that discarded missile system.*

Baker Spring, "Countering North Korea's Missiles: The Missile Defense System the
U.S. Should Have," *Heritage Foundation Web Memo #1138*, June 21, 2006. www.heri
tage.org. Reproduced by permission.

As you read, consider the following questions:

1. Why is the current U.S. missile defense system weak, according to Spring?
2. As the author describes, what is the Brilliant Pebbles element of the GPALS defense plan?
3. In 1991, what was the estimated cost of implementing the GPALS defense system, according to Spring?

Since early May [2006], North Korea has been preparing for a potential missile launch, which now appears imminent [and was eventually tried in July 2006]. In response, Americans are debating how the United States should respond to such a launch. At this point, several facts are clear. First, the North Korean threat underscores the importance of a comprehensive national missile defense system, capable of defending America and her allies. Second, North Korea—or any rogue nation which refuses to abide by the customs of civilized society—should not be allowed to engage in threatening, unannounced missile launches. Finally, some have suggested the United States should launch a preemptive strike at the North Korean missile launch pad. This course of action may indeed be justifiable if it was determined that the launch was threatening—if, for example, a nuclear warhead was placed on the missile.

Short of such an explicit threat, the U.S. should take the middle ground by engaging its missile defense system. Within seconds of a North Korean launch, American sensors could analyze the missile's trajectory and determine whether purpose—most likely either a satellite deployment or an Intercontinental Ballistic Missile (ICBM). If the launch appears to be of an ICBM, the United States should use its missile defense system to destroy the missile.

U.S. Missile System Is Operational

According to news reports, the Department of Defense has already put the nation's developmental missile defense system in operational status in response to the North Korean preparations. This is a wise response because the military must be prepared to defend any threat to the lives and property of Americans posed by North Korea's prospective missile launch, whether that threat comes in the form of an intentional attack or as a consequence of an errant flight. Likewise, the U.S. will need to fulfill its treaty obligations to its allies such as Australia, Japan, and South Korea if North Korea's actions threaten their sovereignty or vital interests. In order to enhance its defensive options, the U.S. needs to intensify its efforts in building a missile defense system.

The defensive option provides a middle ground between preemptively destroying a missile launch site and waiting to retaliate after the loss of life and destruction of property. The U.S. military could destroy a launch site prior to launch, but this would be difficult, although not impossible, to justify. Moreover, a preemptive strike could lead to a large-scale military conflict. Nevertheless, if the [George W.] Bush Administration could convincingly demonstrate that North Korea had mated its missile to a nuclear warhead and was, therefore, intending to launch a purposeful attack, then the preemptive option would be warranted and necessary. A retaliatory response, on the other hand, accepts the potential loss of life and property and assumes, perhaps inaccurately, that a North Korean action warrants retaliation. Arguing that the U.S. should undertake military retaliation in response to destruction resulting from what is later shown to be an errant missile test is problematic. A retaliatory strike, like a preemptive strike, also carries the significant risk of a broader military conflict.

A Very Limited Defense

Congress and the American people, however, need to understand that the missile defense system, particularly for countering long-range missiles of the sort North Korea is reportedly

Obstacles to U.S. Offensive Strategy vs. North Korea

[North Korean] nuclear installations . . . constitute tough nuts to crack. Targeting problems would be tremendous, since intelligence reports are sketchy. Prospects for success would be uncertain even if available data were perfect and preemptive strikes achieved pinpoint accuracy against exposed targets, such as cooling systems, power supplies, and the main [plutonium] processing plant at Yongbyon. Direct hits by conventional munitions that breach the core of active reactors could cover Seoul with radioactive fallout within a few hours and perhaps southern Japan the next day. Subterranean installations defy easy obliteration, because entrances commonly are concealed in steep-sided ravines. Terminally-guided, earth-penetrating bombs and terrain-hugging cruise missiles, hard pressed to make necessarily sharp turns in such close quarters, might temporarily block access and egress routes with landslides, but nuclear weapons protected by bedrock likely would remain intact.

John M. Collins, U.S. Naval Institute Proceedings, *November 2006.*

prepared to launch, represents a very limited capability. First, the missile defense system is still in development, and it has an embedded operational capability because the system has to be built in order to test it. Second, there are only eleven ground-based interceptors—nine fielded in Alaska and two in California—capable of intercepting long-range missiles. According to the Director of the Missile Defense Agency, Lt. General Henry A. Obering, in his March 9, 2006, testimony before the Strategic Forces Subcommittee of the House Armed Services Committee, the Navy is seeking to field up to 20 Standard Missile-3 (SM-3) interceptors on four Aegis ships by the end of [2006]. These missiles, however, are currently designed to counter medium-range missiles. These interceptors are backed by a variety of sensors and radar to detect and track missiles in flight and a command and control network for operating the system.

Given the very limited capabilities of this defense, the ability of the system to intercept and destroy a North Korean missile in flight does not provide an assured defense, even under circumstances favorable to the defense. If the North Korean missile is a long-range missile headed toward Alaska or the West Coast, the ground-based interceptors in Alaska and California are capable of performing an intercept. If the long-range missile is launched toward U.S. ally Australia, the ground-based interceptors are not well positioned to perform an intercept. If the missile turns out to be a medium-range missile and is launched over the ocean—for example, in the direction of the U.S. territory of Guam or U.S. ally Japan—the SM-3 missile has the theoretical capability of performing an intercept. The actual capability depends on the location of the ship carrying SM-3 interceptors at the time of the North Korean missile launch, and so it is impossible to state precisely the likelihood of success. Nevertheless, an intercept attempt is appropriate when it is likely that the unimpeded launch is threatening to the U.S. or jeopardizes the supreme interests of a U.S. ally.

The Abandoned GPALS Plan

Congress and the American people may understandably be uncomfortable with the limited missile defense capabilities available today. Today's missile defense capabilities could be much stronger. On February 12, 1991, the Director of the Strategic Defense Initiative Organization, Ambassador Henry F. Cooper, and the Assistant Secretary of Defense for International Security Policy, Stephen J. Hadley (now National Security Advisor to President Bush), provided a briefing to the press and public on the Global Protection Against Limited

Strikes (GPALS) missile defense plan. The plan was based on the analysis of the trends in the development and deployment of ballistic missiles throughout the world at that time. In hindsight the basis of the plan is justified by North Korea's ballistic missile capabilities today. At least a portion of the significant elements of the GPALS missile defense architecture would be operational today if Congress and the [Bill] Clinton administration had not abandoned the plan in 1991.

GPALS would have been capable of defending against up to 200 individual missile reentry vehicles. The architecture would have included a family of defensive interceptors for countering short- and medium-range missiles, ground-based missile defenses for countering long-range ballistic missiles launched at U.S. territory in far larger numbers than the 11 available today, as well as being operational, a broader and more robust sensor network and command and control system and a constellation of space-based interceptors called Brilliant Pebbles. The Brilliant Pebbles interceptors would have provided a defense against most short-range and all long-range ballistic missiles. Further, the constellation would have had the theoretical capability of countering long-range missiles launched from anywhere in the world against any target in the world. The actual capability ultimately depended on the numbers and deployment pattern of the interceptors. Taken as a whole, this architecture would have also allowed multiple shots at the kind of missile North Korea is prepared to test. The acquisition cost of GPALS system was estimated in 1991 to be approximately $41 billion in 1988 dollars.

Even if the full numbers of each element of the GPALS architecture were not deployed today, it would still cover the full scope of potential targets of a North Korea missile attack, including U.S. territory and the territory of U.S. friends and allies. This includes a missile carrying countermeasures and decoys designed to overwhelm the defense. The confidence level in countering a single missile would be far higher than it is today.

Giving the Nation More Defensive Options

A defensive option against missile attack is essential to a balanced U.S. military posture in facing the kind of threat posed by North Korea today. It provides the president with a wider variety of military options in a world where both nuclear weapons and ballistic missile delivery systems are proliferating and future events are difficult to predict. The other military options available to the president, specifically the preemptive and retaliatory options, are currently robust. The defensive option, however, continues to lag.

If the North Koreans launch a threatening ICBM, the president should act in defense of the country and shoot it down. Moreover, it is long past time for this Congress to take the steps that its predecessor and the Clinton administration should have taken in the early 1990s and put a missile defense architecture similar to GPALS in place. North Korea has provided a reason why this is necessary.

> *"The president needs to act swiftly to eliminate North Korea's nuclear program—through intense bilateral diplomacy."*

The United States Should Negotiate with North Korea to Turn Back Its Nuclear Agenda

Susan E. Rice

In the following viewpoint, Susan E. Rice argues that the United States must pursue serious bilateral talks with North Korea if it intends to slow or stop the North Korean plan to build nuclear weapons. Rice maintains that the United States does not have the military strength to invade North Korea nor would the U.S. government be comfortable in accepting a nuclear rogue state, so the best option is to engage in negotiations that are backed with guaranteed diplomatic and economic incentives. Susan E. Rice is a senior fellow in foreign policy studies at the Brookings Institution, an independent research organization.

As you read, consider the following questions:

1. According to Rice, what are the three options America can pursue in response to North Korea's nuclear agenda?

2. What are the two elements of the U.S. nuclear containment strategy, as the author defines them?

3. Why does Rice believe there is nothing for America to lose in starting bilateral talks with North Korea?

"That horse is out of the barn," said actor and former Republican senator Fred Thompson when asked about North Korea's nuclear program. Thompson spoke at the premiere of *Last Best Chance*, a chillingly realistic film sponsored by the Nuclear Threat Initiative. In it, he plays a president who fails to prevent [the terrorist group] al Qaeda from smuggling stolen nukes into the United States, dramatizing the imperative to halt proliferation at its source.

President [George W.] Bush agrees that the greatest threat we face is nuclear weapons in the hands of terrorists. If, indeed, the North Korean horse "is out of the barn," we face a grave risk. To date, President Bush has failed to prevent North Korea from producing enough fissile material to build an estimated six to eight nuclear weapons, up from one to two in 2003.

Though administration officials have played down the significance of North Korea's growing arsenal, the threat to the United States has greatly increased. Impoverished North Korea now probably has enough nuclear material to sell its surplus to the highest bidder and still retain its own stockpile. Al Qaeda, which aims to use weapons of mass destruction against the United States, could be that bidder.

We face an urgent crisis. In [mid-2005] North Korea has declared that it has nuclear weapons, has prepared to harvest plutonium sufficient for two more bombs and has hinted that it might conduct a nuclear test. If North Korea tests a nuclear weapon, there is little hope of reversing its nuclear program or of averting a regional arms race. [North Korea tested a nuclear weapon in 2006.]

Negotiations Were Working

The North Korean bomb is a disaster that did not have to happen. It represents a failure of U.S. foreign policy. When the [George W.] Bush administration came into office, North Korea had enough material for only one or two bombs. It had agreed in 1994 to freeze its existing nuclear program and accept on-site international monitoring. That agreement was partially successful, contrary to what President Bush has claimed. During most of the 1990's the North Korean nuclear program remained under inspected lockdown. When that agreement began to unravel after 1998, the [Bill] Clinton administration negotiated a new arrangement in its final months of office to halt North Korea's missile tests and nuclear weapons development in exchange for a U.S. commitment to normalize economic and diplomatic relations. The Bush administration refused to carry on the negotiations, however. The White House rejected direct talks with Pyongyang [the North Korean capital] and resorted instead to name-calling, labeling the regime part of the "axis of evil."

David Cortright, America,
December 11, 2006.

America's Options

At this late stage, the United States has three options.

First, we could strike North Korea's suspected nuclear facilities or use force to change the regime. Military options must remain on the table, but all of them are problematic. U.S. intelligence on North Korea is poor. Overstretched in Iraq, the United States does not have ground forces for an invasion. South Korea and China vehemently oppose military action. Worse still, North Korea could retaliate with a nuclear or conventional strike on nearby Seoul, on our more than 30,000 U.S. troops in South Korea, on Japan or even on the United States.

Second, we could accept a nuclear North Korea. But its erratic leader, Kim Jong Il, could still try to sell excess fissile material. He may also have the ability to attach a nuclear warhead to a long-range missile and hit the continental United States. Unfortunately, containment depends on two unreliable tools: national missile defense, which tests have proved is still hit-or-miss, and the proliferation security initiative—a seaborne, needle-in-the-haystack search complicated further by the refusal of China and South Korea to participate.

Third, the United States could pursue intensive bilateral negotiations within the framework of the Chinese-led six-party talks. Having dubbed North Korea and Iran charter members of the "axis of evil," the administration trades insults with those regimes while rejecting direct negotiations with "tyrants" and cheaters as repugnant. They are indeed, but not nearly as repugnant as a nuclear attack by terrorists on an American city.

The United States Needs to Bargain

The president should recognize that rolling back North Korea's nuclear program is more important to U.S. national security than any principled objection to direct negotiations or tacit ambitions to change that odious regime. He should immediately propose high-level, bilateral talks and personally confirm that the United States has "no hostile intent" toward North Korea. In exchange for the "complete, verifiable and irreversible" dismantling of North Korea's nuclear programs, the United States should offer security guarantees, economic ties, fuel supplies and diplomatic relations.

At this eleventh hour, North Korea might refuse the bilateral talks it has long sought, or such negotiations could well fail. Yet a serious effort to negotiate is critical to any hope of gaining eventual South Korean or Chinese assent to punitive action. If direct negotiations fail, President Bush will merely face the same choice he does today: launch a potentially catastrophic war on the Korean Peninsula or allow North Korea to expand its nuclear arsenal, hoping we can catch any bombs it might sell before they cross our borders.

There is speculation that the administration may decide to seek U.N. sanctions against North Korea and, if China vetoes them or refuses to exert major pressure, blame China for this crisis. Primary responsibility rests with North Korea, but for too long the administration has relegated the problem to the sidelines and subcontracted U.S. policy to China, whose interests differ substantially from ours. To now blame China or seek unattainable sanctions would be posturing, not responsible policy.

Time is not on our side. The president needs to act swiftly to eliminate North Korea's nuclear program—through intense bilateral diplomacy. A continued refusal to try would squander our "last best chance" to salvage a nightmarish policy failure.

Periodical Bibliography

The following articles have been selected to supplement the diverse views presented in this chapter.

Russ Feingold	"American National Security and Finishing the Mission in Iraq," *Vital Speeches of the Day*, September 1, 2005.
Noah Feldman	"Islam, Terror and the Second Nuclear Age," *New York Times Magazine*, October 29, 2006.
Steve Forbes	"We Can Still Win in Iraq," *Forbes*, February 12, 2007.
Yossi Klein Halevi and Michael B. Oren	"Contra Iran," *New Republic*, February 5, 2007.
Daniel Henninger	"Talking Ourselves into Defeat," *Wall Street Journal*, January 25, 2007.
Mark Hosenball	"How Close Is Iran to Having Nuclear Weapons?" *Newsweek*, September 25, 2006.
Oliver North	"Contain North Korea," *Human Events*, October 16, 2006.
Ronald E. Powaski	"North Korea's Nuclear Challenge," *America*, February 12, 2007.
Chitra Ragavan, Danielle Burton, and Stephanie A. Salmon	"Who Lost Iraq?" *U.S. News & World Report*, November 27, 2006.
Mark Steyn	"Look to the Wider War," *National Review*, January 29, 2007.
Fareed Zakaria	"Losing the War, as Well as the Battle," *Newsweek*, December 25, 2006.
Stephen Zunes	"The Iranian Nuclear Threat," *Tikkun*, January/February 2007.

CHAPTER 3

Are U.S. Homeland Security Measures Effectively Countering Terrorism?

Chapter Preface

In December 2001, President George W. Bush made a few unguarded remarks that revealed his authorization of a National Security Agency (NSA) program to intercept the international phone, e-mail, and other communications of U.S. citizens. The Terrorist Surveillance Program (TSP), Bush later explained, was created shortly after the September 11, 2001, terrorist attacks and is supposedly targeted at only those people in the United States who are suspected of communicating with terrorist operatives outside the country. After repeated calls for clarification of what materials had been gathered, the president refused to shed light on who was being targeted and what data were being collected, because such answers would jeopardize state security.

In January 2006, several civil rights organizations headed by the American Civil Liberties Union (ACLU) filed suit against the National Security Agency claiming that the TSP was unconstitutional. The ACLU argued that the government was given the power to wiretap U.S. citizens to gather foreign intelligence only through the mandates of court warrants as prescribed by the Foreign Intelligence Surveillance Act of 1978 (FISA) and administered by the Foreign Intelligence Surveillance Court (FISC). The Bush administration had not sought warrants to conduct its various interceptions because the number of wiretaps, the movement of suspects, and the bureaucracy of obtaining court approval would, in their view, take too long. The U.S. attorney general has also stated that obtaining warrants—which he felt the administration could easily get—would compromise state secrets. The attorney general further asserted that the president was acting within his powers to authorize NSA wiretaps chiefly because Congress gave him permission to use any means necessary to pursue terrorists when it passed the Authorization for Use of Military Force (AUMF) bill immediately following the September attacks.

In August 2006, a Detroit district court judge ruled in favor of the ACLU, stating that the TSP was unconstitutional and a violation of the FISA protocols. That judgment is being appealed, and the government has been given approval by the appellate court to continue its program until the appeal is heard. In the meantime, two Democratic senators, Patrick Leahy and Edward Kennedy, sponsored a Senate resolution that denied that the intention of the AUMF had been to grant the government the powers to spy on U.S. citizens. Others in the Senate and the House of Representatives, however, proposed a series of bills that would specifically grant the president the powers he had assumed as well as excuse past warrantless surveillance with a congressional amnesty. None of these had been ratified before Congress recessed in late 2006. And before the issue could be raised again, the Bush administration struck a deal with the FISC to get rapid approval for its TSP activities. Neither the president nor the court is acknowledging what the terms of this deal are or what powers have been granted. Some senators are suspicious of this development and are proposing legislation that would enact some form of oversight of the TSP and the administration's newly brokered deal.

Senator Russ Feingold is one of the senators who still believe the NSA wiretapping programs are illegal. Feingold is just one of the commentators featured in the following chapter that focuses on controversial homeland security measures.

> *"[The Department of Homeland Security is] improving the flow of two-way information and fusing our intelligence—not only horizontally across the government, but vertically at all levels, as well."*

U.S. Homeland Security Is Improving

Michael Chertoff

Former appellate judge and former assistant U.S. attorney general Michael Chertoff was confirmed as the secretary of the Department of Homeland Security (DHS) in February 2005. In the following viewpoint, Chertoff analyzes the accomplishments of the department during the initial years of his tenure. Chertoff asserts that the DHS is employing new technologies to secure the nation's borders, working with allies to apprehend terrorists, and organizing effective responses to any emergency that occurs on American soil. Chertoff states that interagency communication is the key to making the nation secure and ensuring rapid response to emerging crises, and he insists that the DHS is working to facilitate better command and control.

Michael Chertoff, "Remarks by Homeland Security Secretary Michael Chertoff on Protecting the Homeland: Meeting Challenges and Looking Forward," Department of Homeland Security, December 14, 2006. www.dhs.gov.

As you read, consider the following questions:

1. What are the three transformative events that Chertoff says has challenged the DHS in recent years?

2. In what way has the DHS improved its immigration and fingerprint databases, according to the author?

3. What does Chertoff say have been some of the obstacles to command-level interoperability in post–September 11 America?

As I look back over two years, or almost two years, in office, I have to say there have been three transformative experiences for the Department of Homeland Security [DHS] and for those of my colleagues who work within it.

The first of these was the intense national spotlight that was turned on the issue of immigration. This problem has been around for decades, but in the last couple of years, . . . it has received a degree of public attention on a sustained basis that I don't think has ever been the case previously.

A second transformative experience for the department was the terrorist plot in London [in] August [2006], which was directed against international airliners flying from the United Kingdom to the United States. This was, by any measure, the most sophisticated plot against the United States that came near to fruition since September 11th [2001]. It tested our ability to share information and to rapidly adjust security measures in the face of a very large-scale, potential attack against the United States. It was a measure of how far we've come since September 11th.

And the third transformative event was Hurricane Katrina, which struck [in August 2005] within a few months after I arrived at the department. It tested our department's preparedness, in fact preparedness at all levels of government. And it tested our ability to respond in myriad and in some respects unimaginable ways.

Each of these transformative experiences challenged our department and our government in the area of homeland security. And we have matured as a result. Let me talk briefly about each of these.

Securing America's Borders

As I've said, immigration has been around for at least 30 years as a public issue. But it has not, in my experience, received the fevered pitch of attention that it's gotten in the last couple of years at any previous period of time.

In order to look at this problem to try to see if we could turn it around and resolve it once and for all, we realized we had to take as a department a sustained, system-based view of the problem of immigration because it's not just a question of more boots on the ground, or more technology, or tougher enforcement in the interior, or changing the rules with respect to immigrant workers. It's about all of those things. It's about understanding the system as a comprehensive whole.

And that's why we came up with the Secure Border Initiative [SBI], which is the implementation of the President's [George W. Bush's] commitment to comprehensive immigration reform, something that addresses the entirety of the problem from the border itself all through the interior of the country and touching upon the very significant economic engine that fuels the vast majority of illegal migration.

Among the things we did to implement this comprehensive approach in the last two years w[as] ending catch-and-release at the border. You'll recall that was a promise I think I made even here when I spoke a year ago, and it was directed at a pernicious and demoralizing policy under which non-Mexicans who could not simply be returned to Mexico were released because we did not have the ability to detain them before we sent them back home. Not only did that undercut the enforcement effort of our Border Patrol, but it sent the signal to people seeking to come into the country illegally that if they were able to make it in, they had a high likelihood of being released even if they were caught. And that was, of course, a very perverse incentive. So we analyzed the system. We applied the resources and since the summer [of 2006] we have ended catch-and-release at the border.

We launched the SBI *Net* contract, an unheralded and unprecedented comprehensive technology approach to getting full situational awareness at the border and to giving the Border Patrol the tools they need to characterize intrusions into the country and to respond effectively. We're going to begin the first phase of this in 28 miles, starting at the very beginning of [2007]. And that's going to complement the President's commitment to double the Border Patrol to over 18,000 by the end of 2008.

In the meantime, as you know, we have had the National Guard join us at the border. And so we are beginning to see the first real results of a comprehensive approach to dealing with the challenge of illegal migration. Using metrics such as the number of apprehensions and what we see on the south side of the border in terms of activity and staging areas, the Border Patrol has informed me that we have seen measurable progress in the last two quarters of fiscal year 2006, as compared with the same time periods in the prior year.

These metrics of progress—apprehensions, ending catch-and-release, and . . . much more vigorous enforcement in the interior, including a dramatic increase in criminal penalties against those who willfully violate the immigration laws, show that when we apply a comprehensive strategy, we can start to produce real results.

But of course, not all of this is within the power of the department or even the executive branch. To develop a truly comprehensive solution, we must put into place the final piece of comprehensive immigration strategy, and that is a temporary worker program. Only a temporary worker program will give us the ability to deal with that tremendous economic draw which has time and again over the years defeated all the enforcement measures that the government has placed on the border to try to get security for this country. And so we look forward to working with Congress [in 2007] to put the final piece of comprehensive immigration reform into place.

The London Plot Failed

Now, on August 10th, [2006,] many of you awoke and turned on your television and your radio to learn of a dramatic plot that had been disrupted in the United Kingdom, a plot in which al Qaeda–linked individuals sought to get on airplanes destined [for] the United States and to detonate those airplanes while they were en route from the United Kingdom.

Behind the scenes, in addition to all the very fine intelligence work and enforcement work done by our British partners and done in cooperation with our intelligence agencies and with our law enforcement folks, there was a tremendous amount of work that needed to be done to totally revamp the security procedures at our airports in the period of six hours between the time we were able to communicate to TSA [Transportation Security Administration] what the true security situation was—because we couldn't obviously put at risk operations that were highly secret—and the time that people were going to start boarding airplanes the following morning under a brand new and much tougher regime of security measures. We had to redesign the program. We had to make sure that the screeners in the six-hour period were adequately educated about what the new rules would be. We had to harmonize with our counterparts in London and all across Europe. And we succeeded in doing this in a way that after the first day caused essentially no disruption in the amount of waiting time and the amount of inconvenience to the traveling public.

This was, I think, a signal accomplishment of the maturation of TSA and the department. This highly classified operation was kept secret until the very last moment, and then in that intervening night, we all pulled all-nighters to be able to get our entire system retooled so that we could efficiently and safely allow the traveling public to travel internationally while we were taking this plot down in the United Kingdom. That is both a sobering reminder of the fact that we still face threats of enormous magnitude, but reflects great credit upon all the lessons we've learned [since 2001] about how to turn security around efficiently, effectively and quietly when we need to do so.

Facing Hurricane Katrina

And finally, [in 2005] we suffered the blow of Katrina, followed very closely thereafter by the blows of Rita and Wilma in what was a uniquely devastating hurricane season for the United States. It forced us to focus on the fact that this country had not adequately planned for a true catastrophe, whether it be a natural catastrophe, or a man-made catastrophe, that the kind of rigorous planning at all levels and the building of capabilities that were necessary in the admittedly rare catastrophic instance was not there. And therefore, although there was tremendous work done by, for example, the Coast Guard in conducting 33,000 rescues, it was a vivid demonstration of the fact that improvisation is no substitute for preparation.

Since that period of time, we've embarked on a very ambitious program of retooling FEMA [Federal Emergency Management Agency] to make it a 21st-century response organization that includes a comprehensive review and adaptation of emergency plans, including a great deal of work that was done to get ourselves prepared in the event we had another serious hurricane season in 2006. It meant a much-strengthened partnership with the Department of Defense for the first time ever in this country's history, joint planning—preparing in advance mission assignments for the Department of Defense to be able to quickly and effectively come to assist civilian authorities in a way that was not—for which the capability was not there before 2006; these are measurable steps forward. And they're important steps forward. But I also have to say we've got a lot more work to do.

We've got to continue to build out our total asset visibility. And we've got to do a much better job, frankly, of how we manage the process of recovery. We still have tens of thousands of people who suffer the lingering effects of Katrina. And as the city of New Orleans and as the state of Mississippi and the state of Louisiana try to recover and rebuild in what is a mammoth task, we have to make sure that FEMA does not become so enmeshed in its own bureaucratic processes sometimes that they lose sight of the need to have simple common sense and humanity in dealing with the public. So we're going to have to continue to crack down and make sure we get this job done.

Rising to the Challenge of Homeland Security

Whether it be, therefore, in the area of immigration, or in the area of managing an international airline threat, or in building a 21st-century response capability, DHS employees over the last two years have exercised enormous perseverance, skill and dedication across a very demanding set of responsibilities.

And just to touch on a couple of other areas where we've had some real accomplishments this past year, for years we had a very significant backlog in terms of processing those who were eligible for citizenship. We laid down as an objective the elimination of the immigration backlog at Citizenship and Immigration Services [CIS]. And we recognized that that backlog was causing real pain and hardship to millions of people who were waiting for a decision about whether they had met the requirements for American citizenship. I am pleased to say that the backlog within CIS is now gone, and notifications are now being made within months.

Government Rating of Homeland Security Programs

Program Name	Rating	Program Name	Rating
Coast Guard: Ports, Waterways, and Coastal Security	Moderately Effective	Immigration and Customs Enforcement: Detention and Removal	Moderately Effective
Customs and Border Protection: Border Security Inspections and Trade Facilitation	Effective	Immigration and Customs Enforcement: Office of Investigations	Adequate
Federal Emergency Management Agency: Disaster Recovery	Adequate	Science and Technology: Emerging Homeland Security Threat Detection	Moderately Effective
Homeland Security Operations Center	Adequate	Transportation Security Administration: Screener Training	Adequate
Immigration Services	Moderately Effective		

TAKEN FROM: U.S. Office of Management and Budget and other federal agencies, "Federal Programs That Are in the Dept. of Homeland Security Agency," 2006. www.whitehouse.gov/omb/expectmore/agency/024.thml.

We've also improved our immigration databases and our fingerprint databases so that for the first time we have real interoperability in a number of cities between the FBI's law enforcement database and DHS' immigration databases. That is producing real results in terms of allowing local police to identify individuals who have both immigration warrants and law enforcement warrants pending against them.

And we've also made major steps in refashioning our intelligence collection and sharing activities of the department under the leadership of our chief intelligence officer, Charlie Allen.

And we're now working very intensively with state and local officials to set up 20 intelligence fusion centers across the country. These centers, which we've funded with about $380 million, will have embedded DHS analysts in state and local offices and also state and local analysts at DHS, improving the flow of two-way information and fusing our intelligence—not only horizontally across the government, but vertically at all levels, as well.

All of these accomplishments are a true testament to the remarkable talent of well over 180,000 DHS employees who face immense challenges every day protecting our borders on land and in coastal waters; analyzing intelligence 24 hours a day, seven days a week; protecting air travelers during extremely busy travel seasons and responding to fires and hurricanes and earthquakes and other natural disasters that often put their own lives in danger. These hardworking men and women of DHS deserve our gratitude for these and so many efforts. . . .

Building 21st-Century Response Capabilities

So that's looking back at some of the challenges and accomplishments that have matured our department. But our work is not done. So what are we going to set as our goals and priorities for the next two years?

I'd like to break these into five categories: First, we've got to protect Americans against dangerous people; second, we've got to protect Americans against dangerous things; third, we've got to make sure that our critical infrastructure is sufficiently hardened so that even if dangerous people or dangerous things are used in an attack, we can resist that attack—we have to build 21st-century response capabilities; and finally, we have to unify the department into a seamless whole, one in which people are both parts of proud components with real legacies, but also working together to build a visionary new 21st-century government organization. . . .

And finally, as we talk about the issue of 21st-century response, let me focus on one particular challenge that I think we've been talking about [since 2001], and that is interoperability. One of the dramatic lessons of 9/11 was the cost in human life when we do not have at least command-level interoperability in cities and in regions. We have, in fact, made a significant amount of progress. There now exists technology—gateway technology—that does allow command-level communication among different kinds of first responders and different kinds of jurisdictions, even if they're using different frequencies. But we also know that there are some obstacles to getting to the level of interoperability that I think we want to achieve.

Some of it is governance, getting all the players to sit at the table and agree on what the rules of the road are going to be. And some of it is giving clear guidance with respect to the next generation of technology, so people can begin to make acquisitions that will migrate to a level of technology that is really befitting the 21st century.

So what we are doing is completing a survey of 75 high-threat regions and issuing a scorecard as to what the gaps are and what the shortfalls are. And that's going to be done within the next few weeks, by the end of [2006]. With that in mind, and with the technology available for both a short-term fix, we're going to push forward to closing those gaps by the end of calendar year 2008. And frankly, a good deal of our effort in terms of pushing out money for grants in the next year or two is going to be focused on this issue of interoperability. This is a challenge we've made a lot of progress in addressing, but we ought to close the gap between where we are now and our final end-state as quickly as possible. . . .

Personal Responsibility

People ask sometimes, what do we envision with a change of control in Congress [after the Democrats won the majority in November 2006]? And there's been a lot of talk about increased oversight. I welcome increased oversight, because I welcome debate about the fundamental strategy that we are undertaking in homeland security. This is a set of decisions the American people, in their entirety, must own because we will all live with the consequences of these choices.

If we decide we want to bankrupt ourselves for security, we will pay the price of that bankruptcy. But if, on the other hand, we begin to heed some of the arguments I've lately read that somehow our concern about homeland security is overblown, that terrorism is really only a "rather limited threat," that terrorism "should be treated essentially as a criminal problem," if we start to heed that argument, then I feel we're going to feel consequences in the loss of lives on the part of our loved ones, our friends and our acquaintances.

So we need to make sure we define very clearly what is at stake and why we're doing what we're doing. People ask me sometimes, what causes you to lie awake at night? And truthfully, no matter how I express the answer to that question, it all boils down to this: If there is an attack in this country, I'm going to have to look the American public in the eye, I'm going to have to look Congress in the eye, and I'm going to have to, most importantly, look in the eye of the people who lost family members in that attack and account to them about whether we have done everything we reasonably could to prevent that.

So I have a very keen, personal sense of responsibility that I share with all of my colleagues in the Department of Homeland Security, and all across the United States, to make the right decision, the sensible decision, not one that simply says, protect everything in a way that's unrealistic, but one that recognizes the real dangers that we face and advances real solutions to address those real dangers.

So that's, in a nutshell, what keeps me awake at night—my responsibility to do my job, and the responsibility which I share with everybody else in the Department of Homeland Security. It's about balance, it's about clarity, and it's about being sensible.

> "While some important steps have been taken to harden our defenses against terrorist attacks, gaping holes remain in our security net."

U.S. Homeland Security Is Failing

Stephen Flynn (Part I) and The New York Times (Part II)

The Department of Homeland Security (DHS) was created in the wake of September 11, 2001, to protect against terrorist attacks and other emergencies on American soil. In Part I of the following viewpoint, Stephen Flynn, a senior fellow in National Security Studies at the Council on Foreign Relations, explains that because the DHS is a relatively new agency, it has many obstacles to overcome in order to fulfill its mission. Flynn says that the department has limited resources, unskilled personnel, and no leverage to gain much needed information from other U.S. intelligence networks. In Part II of the viewpoint, an editorial writer for the New York Times *gives several examples of how the DHS is failing to protect ports of entry to the United States and other potential terrorist targets throughout the nation.*

As you read, consider the following questions:

1. Why does Flynn say the DHS must "settle for what it is given" in terms of information gathering?

2. What problems still plague U.S. airline security, according to the *New York Times* editorial?

3. As the *New York Times* reports, how does the 9/11 commission believe homeland security funds should be disbursed to the states?

Part I

While any government reorganization effort promises to be a bumpy ride, the new Department of Homeland Security has had to face a number of start-up hurdles that go beyond run-of-the-mill bureaucratic intransigence. One handicap has been that the department needs to have lots of people with new skills. Today, immigration agents have to be cross-trained in customs laws and inspection protocols. Frontline officers must work with sophisticated technologies and be able to interact with a variety of different people, including those in the private sector. Inspectors are being sent overseas to interact with their counterparts as a part of a broad strategic effort to push America's borders out. There is the need for greater community relations to explain why new measures are being taken and to encourage the public to support those changes. These kinds of skills cannot be developed by relying on the long-standing practice of providing on-the-job training in the field. As a result, meeting the department's new mandate puts an enormous strain on rickety agency personnel systems that were built for simpler jobs in a simpler time.

Beyond the management challenges associated with identifying and meeting new personnel needs, the department has been given agencies that are reluctant to take on ambitious initiatives out of a concern that they barely have the resources to cope with the existing ones. The pace of operations associated with homeland security, particularly when it involves raised alert levels, is generating wear and tear on equipment and people. At the same time, investments to replace obsolete facilities and systems continue to plod along at a glacial pace. For instance, while the ships and aircraft of the Coast Guard are out on more frequent and longer security patrols, the service is still operating on a pre-9/11 acquisition plan that will take up to twenty-seven years to replace its already ancient fleet.

The senior management at the new department must also wrestle with the challenges associated with intruding on the turf of the other departments in the executive branch. For example, new security rules to protect our borders raise important challenges for maintaining the free movement of people and goods. But DHS is not staffed to reach out to other departments on an ongoing basis. Nor do the State, Treasury, Commerce, Transportation, and Agriculture Departments, along with the U.S. Trade Representative, have senior people assigned to focus on the diplomatic, economic, and trade dimensions of dealing with our homeland security agenda. Inevitably, clashes among competing U.S. interests that could have been anticipated and minimized by good upfront coordination turn into bureaucratic brush fires that consume the time and energy of top officials who must endeavor to extinguish them.

One particularly gray area that DHS must sort out is how to interact with the Department of Defense. The Pentagon has been keen to maintain its autonomy by assigning to itself the mission of "homeland defense," which it defines as involving terrorist attacks that emanate only from outside the United States. Relying on this definition, defense planners have essentially found a way to carve out a niche where the armed forces patrol air space and the high seas, and prepare to respond to catastrophic attacks when they happen. While there are some liaison officers assigned to one another's staffs, by and large, the Pentagon, through its new Office of Homeland Defense and Northern Command, is marshalling its considerable expertise and resources to do its own thing.

DHS must also contend with daunting problems associated with trying to gather and distribute the intelligence to support its mission. Historically, intelligence and investigative agencies are unwilling to share classified or sensitive information with bureaucracies that they consider potential competitors for their mission. Then there is the unwritten rule in the intelligence community that you have to give something to get something. The Secretary of Homeland Security has very little to give because DHS has been assigned only the job of analyzing intelligence, not collecting it. One indication of how the intelligence role at DHS is viewed within the federal government is that more than a dozen highly qualified candidates turned down the offer to be the department's intelligence chief. Since DHS exercises no control over the FBI [Federal Bureau of Investigation], CIA [Central Intelligence Agency], and the other federal intelligence agencies, the department has no leverage by which to help shape intelligence collection priorities. As a result, it must settle for what it is given, which invariably is not enough to satisfy the pleadings for better threat information by local, state, and private sector authorities.

Even within the new department there are intimidating technical and procedural barriers to sharing information. One agency is often unable to pass along data to another agency because it is saddled with technology that makes that process very cumbersome. DHS inherited a smorgasbord of old mainframe computer systems that were designed not so much for managing data as for collecting and storing it. There are also legal barriers that must be worked out to get these systems to talk to one another. Congress has always been wary of concentrating too much information at the fingertips of government bureaucrats and has stipulated in statute just what an agency may do with the data it collects.

In short, the internal and intramural struggles the Department of Homeland Security faces within the executive branch are considerable. But Congress presents yet another enormous challenge to the department's ability to focus on its mission because of unresolved issues related to overlapping jurisdictions. In the first ten months of the new department's life, its senior officials testified on 162 occasions in front of twenty-two full committees and thirty-seven subcommittees. Since each committee hearing typically requires twenty-four hours to prepare, the department spent an equivalent of 486 work days to support appearances before the House and Senate. Back at the office, DHS officials had to respond to more than 1,600 letters from members asking for additional information within the same time period. No one would expect Alan Greenspan, the chairman of the Federal Reserve, to report to dozens of committees. Nor would we expect George Tenet, the director of Central Intelligence, and his senior managers to be spending much of their working week testifying before congressional committees.

In theory, only four congressional committees are supposed to be in charge of the homeland security mission: the Senate Committee on Governmental Affairs, the House Select Committee on Homeland Security, and the Senate and House Appropriations committees. The Governmental Affairs Committee has been assigned the homeland security mandate as part of its duties in overseeing the organization of the executive branch. Because of the small size of the Senate, this appears to be working reasonably well. However, in the House of Representatives, the work of the Select Committee is complicated by the fact that it has fifty members, most of whom are powerful chairmen of standing committees. While the select

Selected Examples of Wasteful Homeland Security Spending

- $10,000,000 to Intercity Bus Security to improve security for operators and passengers by providing bus security enhancements and training to bus companies and others

- $22,000,000 to the trucking industry security program to promote security awareness among all segments of the commercial motor carriers and transportation community

- $2.5 billion for "highway security," which consists of building and improving roads

- $50,000,000 to provide an exercise program that meets the intent of the Oil Pollution Act of 1990

- $38 million to fully cover all remaining fire claims from the Cerro Grande Fire in New Mexico

- $20,000,000 to renovate the Nebraska Avenue Headquarters of the Department of Homeland Security

- $22,800 for Mason County, Washington, to buy six radios that are incompatible with county radios

- $30,000 for a Tennessee high school to have a defibrillator on hand for a basketball tournament

- $98,000 for training courses by the Tecumseh, Michigan, fire department—that no one attended

- $557,400 to North Pole, an Alaska town of 1,570 people, for homeland security rescue and communications equipment

Veronique de Rugy, Reason,
March 2006.

Committee has very capable leadership it its chairman, Rep. Christopher Cox (R-CA), and its ranking member Rep. Jim Turner (D-TX), the remaining members seem more intent on ensuring that the new committee does not encroach on their turf, rather than working toward the special committee's mandate. The result is that DHS officials end up practically living on Capitol Hill, responding to legislative inquiries which obviously detracts from the time they could spend doing their primary jobs.

The bottom line is that it will be some time before we can expect Washington's new homeland security bureaucracy to be firing on all cylinders. Given the urgency of the threat, this is worrisome. However, it is not the most pressing issue that confronts us. The bigger challenge lies with identifying how to formally engage the broader civil society and the private sector, not just the federal government, in a national effort to make America a less attractive terrorist target. This is a task that requires a much different kind of institutional framework than one that involves reshuffling agencies within the executive branch. We need to mobilize the homeland by drawing for inspiration on existing entities and practices that work.

Part II

Ever since British intelligence did such a masterly job in rounding up terrorists intent on blowing up airliners [in August 2006], the [George W.] Bush administration has relentlessly tried to divert attention from the disintegration in Iraq and focus instead on its supposed prowess in protecting our country against terrorist attacks. That ploy ought not to wash. While the administration has been pouring its energies and money into Iraq, it has fallen far behind on steps needed to protect the homeland.

You would not know that from listening to the president or other top officials in recent days. In a tour of the National

Counterterrorism Center in Virginia, President Bush declared that "America is safer than it has been" and assured Americans that "we're doing everything in our power to protect you."

If only that were so. The sad truth is that while some important steps have been taken to harden our defenses against terrorist attacks, gaping holes remain in our security net.

Airline Insecurity

For starters, consider aviation, where billions have been spent to improve airline and airport security, with only middling results. The likelihood that terrorists will be able to hijack passenger jets as they did on 9/11 has been greatly reduced by hardening cockpit doors, arming pilots on some routes and placing many more air marshals on flights. The screening of all passengers, their carry-on bags and their checked luggage has also made it much harder to smuggle standard bombs or metallic weapons aboard.

But there is still no system to detect liquid explosives, a shocking deficiency more than a decade after terrorists were caught preparing to use such explosives to bring down a dozen airliners over the Pacific Ocean. The installation of "puffer" machines to detect trace explosives is lagging, and a program to integrate explosive-detection machines into the automated baggage conveyor systems at airports will not be finished, at the current pace of spending, for another 18 years.

Very little of the commercial air cargo that is carried aboard planes is screened or inspected, mostly because neither the shippers nor the airlines want to disrupt this lucrative flow of business. There is still no unified watch list to alert airlines to potentially dangerous passengers, and a prescreening program that would match airline passengers against terrorist watch lists remains stuck in development. All this in the industry that has received the most lavish attention since 9/11.

Unsecured Weapons of Mass Destruction

Even worse gaps remain in other areas. Port security relies primarily on certifying that cargo shipments are safe before they are loaded on freighters headed for this country. Only a small percentage of containers are screened once they hit our shores, raising the fearsome possibility that a nuclear or biological weapon might be smuggled in and detonated here.

Programs to keep dangerous nuclear materials in the former Soviet Union out of the hands of terrorists through greater security are moving so slowly that it will take another 14 years to complete the job. This is reckless beyond belief when nuclear terrorism is the most frightening prospect of all.

On the industrial front, the nation's chemical plants, perhaps the most lethal and vulnerable of all our manufacturing complexes, remain dangerously underdefended, mostly because the government has been unwilling to compel private industry to take action. A new tamper-proof identification card for workers in the far-flung transportation industry has yet to be issued.

Failing Grades

The leaders of the 9/11 commission issued a final report [in] December [2005] analyzing how well the administration and Congress had done in carrying out the commission's 41 recommendations. They awarded only one A minus (for disrupting terrorist financing), a batch of B's and C's, and a dozen D's in such critical areas as reforming intelligence oversight, assessing infrastructure vulnerabilities and sharing information among government agencies. A failure to share intelligence allowed the 9/11 terrorists to succeed despite advance hints of their presence and intentions.

The commission awarded five failing grades, the most serious of them for Washington's failure to allocate homeland security funds based on risk. Even after moderate tinkering with the formulas, greedy legislators from states that face little danger continue to siphon off funds that would be better used to protect New York, Washington and other large cities likely to hold the greatest attraction for terrorists.

Almost everyone agrees that the administration has taken some important steps toward greater security, but as the leaders of the 9/11 commission recently commented, it has not made the issue a top priority. The long, costly, chaotic occupation of Iraq, though touted as a front line of the war on terror, has actually sapped energy, resources and top-level attention that would be better applied to the real threat, a terrorist attack on the homeland.

> *"The purpose of [warrantless wiretapping] is not to collect reams of intelligence, but to detect and prevent attacks."*

Wiretapping Will Protect America from Attack

Michael V. Hayden

In December 2005, President George W. Bush revealed that the National Security Agency (NSA) had been gathering information by scanning communications (phone and e-mail) between suspected terrorists inside and outside the United States. This wiretapping was being conducted without recourse to a federal warrant. Critics argued that such warrantless wiretapping violated the Foreign Intelligence Surveillance Act (FISA) of 1978. The administration, however, argued that the urgency of the times demanded quick and covert action. In the following viewpoint, principal deputy director of national intelligence defends the NSA's eavesdropping, claiming that the department cleared its actions with the president and federal legal advisers. He also contends that this form of wiretapping is not meant to curtail the individual liberties of law-abiding citizens but is solely directed at stopping terrorists.

Michael V. Hayden, "Is the National Security Agency's Domestic Surveillance Program Legal?: Pro and Con," *Congressional Digest*, April 2006, pp. 116–122.

As you read, consider the following questions:

1. What three agencies approved the use of warrantless wiretaps, according to Hayden?
2. As the author explains, what kinds of calls are targeted by warrantless wiretaps?
3. How does Hayden refute claims that the wiretap program is tantamount to "domestic spying"?

N SA intercepts communications, and it does so for only one purpose—to protect the lives, the liberties, and the well-being of the citizens of the United States from those who would do us harm. By the late 1990s, that job was becoming increasingly more difficult. The explosion of modern communications in terms of volume, variety, and velocity threatened to overwhelm us.

The agency took a lot of criticism in those days, I know—criticism that it was going deaf, that it was ossified in its thinking, that it had not and could not keep up with the changes in modern communications. Those were really interesting times. As we were being criticized for being incompetent and going deaf, others seemed to be claiming that we were omniscient and we were reading your emails.

NSA had, NSA has, an existential problem. In order to protect American lives and liberties, it has to be two things: powerful in its capabilities, and secretive in its methods. And we exist in a political culture that distrusts two things most of all: power and secrecy.

Modern communications didn't make this any easier. Gone were the days when signals of interest—that's what NSA calls the things they want to copy—went along some dedicated microwave link between strategic rocket forces headquarters in Moscow and some ICBM [intercontinental ballistic missile] in western Siberia. By the late 1990s, what NSA calls targeted communications—things like al Qaeda [terrorist group] communications—coexisted out there in a great global web with your phone calls and my emails. NSA needed the power to pick out the one, and the discipline to leave the others alone.

So, this question of security and liberty wasn't a new one for us in September 2001. We've always had this question: How do we balance the legitimate need for foreign intelligence with our responsibility to protect individual privacy rights?

It's a question drilled into every employee of NSA from day one, and it shapes every decision about how NSA operates.

NSA Authority Before and After 9/11

September 11 didn't change that. But it did change some things. This ability to intercept communication—we commonly refer to it as Signals Intelligence or SIGINT. SIGINT is a complex business, with operational and technological and legal imperatives often intersecting and overlapping. There's routinely some freedom of action—within the law—to adjust operations. After the attacks, I exercised some options I've always had that collectively better prepared us to defend the homeland.

What is it that NSA does routinely? Where do we set the threshold, for example, for what constitutes inherent foreign intelligence value? That's what we're directed to collect. That's what we're required to limit ourselves to—inherent foreign intelligence value. Where we set that threshold, for example, in reports involving a U.S. person shapes how we do our job, shapes how we collect, shapes how we report.

The American SIGINT system, in the normal course of foreign intelligence activities, inevitably captures this kind of information, information to, from, or about what we call a U.S. person. And by the way, "U.S. person" routinely includes anyone in the United States, citizen or not. So, for example, because they were in the United States—and we did not know anything more—Mohamed Atta and his fellow 18 hijackers would have been presumed to have been protected persons, U.S. persons, by NSA prior to 9/11.

Inherent foreign intelligence value is one of the metrics we must use to ensure that we conform to the Fourth Amendment's reasonable standard when it comes to protecting the privacy of these kinds of people. . . .

Prior to September 11, airline passengers were screened in one way. After September 11, we changed how we screen passengers. In the same way, although prior to September 11 certain communications weren't considered valuable intelligence, it became immediately clear after September 11 that intercepting and reporting these same communications were in fact critical to defending the homeland.

Getting Authorization and Clearance

Now let me make this point. These decisions were easily within my authorities as the director of NSA under Executive Order 12333, signed in 1981, an Executive order that has governed NSA for nearly a quarter-century.

Let me summarize. In the days after 9/11, NSA was using its authorities and its judgment to appropriately respond to the most catastrophic attack on the homeland in the history of the Nation. That shouldn't be a headline, but as near as I can tell, these actions on my part have created some of the noise in recent press coverage. Let me be clear on this point— except that they involved NSA, these programs were not related to the authorization that the President [George W. Bush] has recently spoken about. Back then, September 2001, I asked to update the Congress on what NSA had been doing, and I briefed the entire House Intelligence Committee on the 1st of October on what we had done under our previously existing authorities. . . .

Warrantless Wiretaps

So now, we come to one additional piece of NSA authorities. These are the activities whose existence the President con-

Attorney General Defends Terrorist Surveillance Program

The conflict against al Qaeda is, in fundamental respects, a war of information. We cannot build walls thick enough, fences high enough, or systems strong enough to keep our enemies out of our open and welcoming country. Instead, as the bipartisan 9/11 and WMD [weapons of mass destruction] Commissions have urged, we must understand better who the enemy is and what he is doing. We have to collect the right dots before we can "connect the dots." The terrorist surveillance program allows us to collect more information regarding al Qaeda's plans, and, critically, it allows us to locate al Qaeda operatives, especially those already in the United States and poised to attack. We cannot defend the Nation without such information, as we painfully learned on September 11th. . . .

The terrorist surveillance program is firmly grounded in the President's constitutional authorities. The Constitution charges the President with the primary responsibility for protecting the safety of all Americans, and the Constitution gives the President the authority necessary to fulfill this solemn duty. It has long been recognized that the President's constitutional powers include the authority to conduct warrantless surveillance aimed at detecting and preventing armed attacks on the United States. . . .

If this authority is available in ordinary times, it is even more vital in the present circumstances of our armed conflict with al Qaeda. The President authorized the terrorist surveillance program in response to the deadliest foreign attack on American soil, and it is designed solely to prevent the next al Qaeda attack.

Alberto R. Gonzales, statement to Senate Judiciary Committee at the hearing "Wartime Executive Power and the NSA's Surveillance Authority," February 6, 2006.

firmed several weeks ago [in December 2005]. That authorization was based on an intelligence community assessment of a serious and continuing threat to the homeland. The lawfulness of the actual authorization was reviewed by lawyers at the Department of Justice and the White House and was approved by the attorney general.

Now, you're looking at me up here, and I'm in a military uniform, and frankly, there's a certain sense of sufficiency here—authorized by the President, duly ordered, its lawfulness attested to by the attorney general, and its content briefed to the congressional leadership.

But we all have personal responsibility, and in the end, NSA would have to implement this, and every operational decision the agency makes is made with the full involvement of its legal office. NSA professional career lawyers—and the agency has a bunch of them—have a well-deserved reputation. They're good, they know the law, and they don't let the agency take many close pitches.

And so even though I knew the program had been reviewed by the White House and by the Department of Justice, I asked the three most senior and experienced lawyers in NSA: Our enemy in the global war on terrorism doesn't divide the United States from the rest of the world, the global telecommunications system doesn't make that distinction either, our laws do and should; how did these activities square with these facts?

They reported back to me. They supported the lawfulness of this program. Supported, not acquiesced. This was very important to me. A veteran NSA lawyer, one of the three I asked, told me that a correspondent had suggested to him recently that all of the lawyers connected with this program have been very careful from the outset because they knew there would be a day of reckoning. The NSA lawyer replied to him that that had not been the case. NSA had been so careful, he said— and I'm using his words now here—NSA had been so careful because in this very focused, limited program, NSA had to ensure that it dealt with privacy interests in an appropriate manner. In other words, our lawyers weren't careful out of fear; they were careful out of a heartfelt, principled view that NSA operations had to be consistent with bedrock legal protections.

Finding Links to al Qaeda

In early October 2001, I gathered key members of the NSA workforce in our conference room and I introduced our new operational authority to them. With the historic culture of NSA being what it was and is, I had to do this personally. I told them what we were going to do and why. I also told them that we were going to carry out this program and not go one step further. NSA's legal and operational leadership then went into the details of this new task.

You know, the 9/11 Commission criticized our ability to link things happening in the United States with things that were happening elsewhere. In that light, there are no communications more important to the safety of this country than those affiliated with al Qaeda with one end in the United States. The President's authorization allows us to track this kind of call more comprehensively and more efficiently. The trigger is quicker and a bit softer than it is for a FISA warrant, but the intrusion into privacy is also limited: only international calls and only those we have a reasonable basis to believe involve al Qaeda or one of its affiliates.

The purpose of all this is not to collect reams of intelligence, but to detect and prevent attacks. The intelligence community has neither the time, the resources, nor the legal authority to read communications that aren't likely to protect us, and NSA has no interest in doing so. These are communications that we have reason to believe are al Qaeda communications, a judgment made by American intelligence professionals, not folks like me or political appointees, a judgment made by the American intelligence professionals most trained to understand al Qaeda tactics, al Qaeda communications, and al Qaeda aims.

Their work is actively overseen by the most intense oversight regime in the history of the National Security Agency. The agency's conduct of this program is thoroughly reviewed by the NSA's general counsel and inspector general. The program has also been reviewed by the Department of Justice for compliance with the President's authorization. Oversight also includes an aggressive training program to ensure that all activities are consistent with the letter and the intent of the authorization and with the preservation of civil liberties.

Who Is Targeted and Who Is Not?

Let me talk for a few minutes also about what this program is not. It is not a driftnet over [typical U.S. cities such as] Dearborn or Lackawanna or Freemont grabbing conversations that we then sort out by these alleged keyword searches or datamining tools or other devices that so-called experts keep talking about.

This is targeted and focused. This is not about intercepting conversations between people in the United States. This is hot pursuit of communications entering or leaving America involving someone we believe is associated with al Qaeda. We bring to bear all the technology we can to ensure that this is so. And if there were ever an anomaly, and we discovered that there had been an inadvertent intercept of a domestic-to-domestic call, that intercept would be destroyed and not reported. But the incident, what we call inadvertent collection, would be recorded and reported. But that's a normal NSA procedure. It's been our procedure for the last quarter-century. And as always, as we always do when dealing with U.S. person information. . . . U.S. identities are expunged when they're not essential to understanding the intelligence value of any report. Again, that's a normal NSA procedure.

So let me make this clear. When you're talking to your daughter at State college, this program cannot intercept your conversations. And when she takes a semester abroad to complete her Arabic studies, this program will not intercept your communications.

Let me emphasize one more thing that this program is not—domestic spying. One end of any call targeted under this program is always outside the United States.

American intelligence, and especially American SIGINT, signals intelligence, is the frontline of defense in dramatically changed circumstances, circumstances in which if we fail to do our job well and completely, more Americans will almost certainly die. The speed of operations, the ruthlessness of the enemy, the pace of modern communications have called on us to do things and to do them in ways never before required. We've worked hard to find innovative ways to protect the American people and the liberties we hold dear.

> "Wiretapping American citizens on American soil without the required warrant is in direct contravention of our criminal statutes."

Warrantless Wiretapping Is Illegal

Russ Feingold

The following viewpoint is an excerpt of a speech made by Senator Russ Feingold on the Senate floor concerning President George W. Bush's program of conducting warrantless wiretaps on suspected terrorists in the United States. As Feingold contends, the president's wiretapping is illegal and needs to be stopped. Feingold asserts that the Constitution protects the privacy of Americans from government intrusion, and the president cannot willfully ignore this fact even in extreme circumstances. Feingold points out that the government already has proper channels through which to pursue sanctioned eavesdropping, but the administration has chosen to ignore these routes in some circumstances and, as a result, has imperiled the freedom of all Americans and the legitimacy of the government. Russ Feingold is a Democratic senator from Wisconsin.

Russ Feingold, Senate statement on the President's warrantless wiretapping program, February 7, 2006. www.feingold.senate.gov.

As you read, consider the following questions:

1. According to Feingold, how has Attorney General Alberto Gonzales misled Congress in the wiretapping debate?

2. As the author states, what reason has the administration given for ignoring the FISA procedures to obtain warrants for wiretapping? How does Feingold respond to this explanation?

3. Why is the Gang of Eight oversight committee an inappropriate check on the president's powers, in Feingold's view?

Mr. President [of the Senate], [in January 2006] the President of the United States [George W. Bush] gave his State of the Union address, where he spoke of America's leadership in the world, and called on all of us to "lead this world toward freedom." Again and again, he invoked the principle of freedom, and how it can transform nations, and empower people around the world.

But, almost in the same breath, the President openly acknowledged that he has ordered the government to spy on Americans, on American soil, without the warrants required by law.

The President issued a call to spread freedom throughout the world, and then he admitted that he has deprived Americans of one of their most basic freedoms under the Fourth Amendment—to be free from unjustified government intrusion.

The President was blunt. He said that he had authorized the NSA's [National Security Agency's] domestic spying program, and he made a number of misleading arguments to defend himself. His words got rousing applause from Republicans, and I think even some Democrats.

Breaking the Law

The President was blunt, so I will be blunt: This program is breaking the law, and this President is breaking the law. Not only that, he is misleading the American people in his efforts to justify this program.

How is that worthy of applause? Since when do we celebrate our commander in chief for violating our most basic freedoms, and misleading the American people in the process? When did we start to stand up and cheer for breaking the law? In that moment at the State of the Union, I felt ashamed.

Congress has lost its way if we don't hold this President accountable for his actions.

The President suggests that anyone who criticizes his illegal wiretapping program doesn't understand the threat we face. But we do. Every single one of us is committed to stopping the terrorists who threaten us and our families.

Defeating the terrorists should be our top national priority, and we all agree that we need to wiretap them to do it. In fact, it would be irresponsible not to wiretap terrorists. But we have yet to see any reason why we have to trample the laws of the United States to do it.

The President's decision that he can break the law says far more about his attitude toward the rule of law than it does about the laws themselves.

This goes way beyond party, and way beyond politics. What the President has done here is to break faith with the American people. In the State of the Union, he also said that "we must always be clear in our principles" to get support from friends and allies that we need to fight terrorism. So let's be clear about a basic American principle: When someone breaks the law, when someone misleads the public in an attempt to justify his actions, he needs to be held accountable. The President of the United States has broken the law. The President of the United States is trying to mislead the American people. And he needs to be held accountable.

No Oversight of the President's Actions

Unfortunately, the President refuses to provide any details about this domestic spying program. Not even the full Intelligence committees know the details, and they were specifically set up to review classified information and oversee the intelligence activities of our government. Instead, the President says—"Trust me." . . .

In December [2005], we found out that the President has authorized wiretaps of Americans without the court orders required by law. He says he is only wiretapping people with links to terrorists, but how do we know? We don't. The President is unwilling to let a neutral judge make sure that is the case. He will not submit this program to an independent branch of government to make sure he's not violating the rights of law-abiding Americans.

So I don't want to hear again that this Administration has shown it can be trusted. It hasn't. And that is exactly why the law requires a judge to review these wiretaps.

It is up to Congress to hold the President to account. We held a hearing on the domestic spying program in the Judiciary Committee, where Attorney General [Alberto] Gonzales was a witness. We expect there will be other hearings. That is a start, but it will take more than just hearings to get the job done.

We know that in part because the President's Attorney General has already shown a willingness to mislead the Congress.

Complicit Evasion

At the hearing [on February 6, 2006], I reminded the Attorney General about his testimony during his confirmation hearings in January 2005, when I asked him whether the President had the power to authorize warrantless wiretaps in violation of the criminal law. We didn't know it then, but the President had authorized the NSA program three years before, when the Attorney General was White House Counsel. At his confirmation hearing, the Attorney General first tried to dismiss my question as "hypothetical." He then testified that "it's not the policy or the agenda of this President to authorize actions that would be in contravention of our criminal statutes."

Well, Mr. President, wiretapping American citizens on American soil without the required warrant is in direct contravention of our criminal statutes. The Attorney General knew that, and he knew about the NSA program when he sought the Senate's approval for his nomination to be Attorney General. He wanted the Senate and the American people to think that the President had not acted on the extreme legal theory that the President has the power as Commander in Chief to disobey the criminal laws of this country. But he had. The Attorney General had some explaining to do, and he didn't do it. Instead he parsed words, arguing that what he said was truthful because he didn't believe that the President's actions violated the law.

But he knew what I was asking, and he knew he was misleading the Committee in his response. If he had been straightforward, he would have told the committee that in his opinion, the President has the authority to authorize warrantless wiretaps. My question wasn't about whether such illegal wiretapping was going on—like almost everyone in Congress, I didn't know about the program then. It was a question about how the nominee to be Attorney General viewed the law. This nominee wanted to be confirmed, and so he let a misleading statement about one of the central issues of his confirmation—his view of executive power—stay on the record until the *New York Times* revealed the program.

The rest of the Attorney General's performance at [that] hearing certainly did not give me any comfort, either. He continued to push the Administration's weak legal arguments, continued to insinuate that anyone who questions this program doesn't want to fight terrorism, and refused to answer basic questions about what powers this Administration is claiming. We still need a lot of answers from this Administration....

Ignoring the Constitution

The President has broken the law, and he has made it clear that he will continue to do so. But the President is not a king. And the Congress is not a king's court. Our job is not to stand up and cheer when the President breaks the law. Our job is to stand up and demand accountability, to stand up and check the power of an out-of-control executive branch.

That is one of the reasons that the framers put us here—to ensure balance between the branches of government, not to act as a professional cheering section.

We need answers. Because no one, not the President, not the Attorney General, and not any of their defenders in this body, has been able to explain why it is necessary to break the law to defend against terrorism. And I think that's because they can't explain it.

Instead, this administration reacts to anyone who questions this illegal program by saying that those of us who demand the truth and stand up for our rights and freedoms have a pre-9/11 view of the world.

In fact, the President has a pre-1776 view of the world.

Our Founders lived in dangerous times, and they risked everything for freedom. Patrick Henry said, "Give me liberty or give me death." The President's pre-1776 mentality is hurting America. It is fracturing the foundation on which our country has stood for 230 years. The President can't just bypass two branches of government, and obey only those laws he wants to obey. Deciding unilaterally which of our freedoms still apply in the fight against terrorism is unacceptable and needs to be stopped immediately....

Wiretapping Has Compromised National Security

First, it has jeopardized the prosecution of alleged terrorists. If evidence obtained under the warrantless surveillance program was or will be used in any criminal prosecutions (as the [George W. Bush] administration has asserted), then those convicted or accused terrorists can and surely will raise a constitutional challenge, potentially irreparably jeopardizing these criminal cases.

Second, the NSA [National Security Agency] program could harm ongoing investigations. The FISA [Foreign Intelligence Surveillance Act] Court, which approves or denies applications for FISA warrants, could shut down any counterterrorism wiretaps that it authorized on the basis of unlawfully collected information. This is not a hypothetical situation. In 2001, the FISA Court shut down numerous wiretaps after learning that the FBI had supplied faulty information in the FISA warrant applications.

Third, ... NSA eavesdropping [has] yielded a tremendous volume of information that led nowhere.

Mark Agrast, Center for American Progress, February 2, 2006.
www.americanprogress.org.

Proper FISA Procedure

The Foreign Intelligence Surveillance Act [FISA] was passed in 1978 to create a secret court, made up of judges who develop national security expertise, to issue warrants for surveillance of terrorists and spies. These are the judges from whom the Bush Administration has obtained thousands of warrants since 9/11. The Administration has almost never had a warrant request rejected by those judges. They have used the FISA Court thousands of times, but at the same time they assert that FISA is an "old law" or "out of date" and they can't comply with it. Clearly they can and do comply with it—except when they don't. Then they just arbitrarily decide to go around these judges, and around the law.

The Administration has said that it ignored FISA because it takes too long to get a warrant under that law. But we know that in an emergency, where the Attorney General believes that surveillance must begin before a court order can be obtained, FISA permits the wiretap to be executed immediately as long as the government goes to the court within 72 hours. The Attorney General has complained that the emergency provision does not give him enough flexibility, he has complained that getting a FISA application together or getting the necessary approvals takes too long. But the problems he has cited are bureaucratic barriers that the executive branch put in place, and could easily remove if it wanted.

FISA also permits the Attorney General to authorize unlimited warrantless electronic surveillance in the United States during the 15 days following a declaration of war, to allow time to consider any amendments to FISA required by a wartime emergency. That is the time period that Congress specified. Yet the President thinks that he can do this indefinitely.

In the State of the Union, the President also argued that federal courts had approved the use of presidential authority that he was invoking. But that turned out to be misleading as well. When I asked the Attorney General about this, he could point me to no court—not the Supreme Court or any other court—that has considered whether, after FISA was enacted, the President nonetheless had the authority to bypass it and authorize warrantless wiretaps. Not one court. The Administration's effort to find support for what it has done in snippets of other court decisions would be laughable if this issue were not so serious.

The President's Admission

The President knows that FISA makes it a crime to wiretap Americans in the United States without a warrant or a court order. Why else would he have assured the public, over and over again, that he was getting warrants before engaging in domestic surveillance?

Here's what the President said on April 20, 2004: "Now, by the way, any time you hear the United States government talking about wiretap, it requires—a wiretap requires a court order. Nothing has changed, by the way. When we're talking about chasing down terrorists, we're talking about getting a court order before we do so."

And again, on July 14, 2004: "The government can't move on wiretaps or roving wiretaps without getting a court order."

The President was understandably eager in these speeches to make it clear that under his administration, law enforcement was using the FISA Court to obtain warrants before wiretapping. That is understandable, since wiretapping Americans on American soil without a warrant is against the law.

And listen to what the President said on June 9, 2005: "Law enforcement officers need a federal judge's permission to wiretap a foreign terrorist's phone, a federal judge's permission to track his calls, or a federal judge's permission to search his property. Officers must meet strict standards to use any of these tools. And these standards are fully consistent with the Constitution of the U.S."

Now that the public knows about the domestic spying program, he has had to change course. He has looked around for arguments to cloak his actions. And all of them are completely threadbare. . . .

Looking for Legitimization

The President's claims of inherent executive authority, and his assertions that the courts have approved this type of activity, are baseless.

The President has argued that periodic internal executive branch review provides an adequate check on the program. He has even characterized this periodic review as a safeguard for civil liberties. But we don't know what this check involves. And we do know that Congress explicitly rejected this idea of unilateral executive decision-making in this area when it passed FISA.

Finally, the president has tried to claim that informing a handful of congressional leaders, the so-called Gang of Eight,[1] somehow excuses breaking the law. Of course, several of these members said they weren't given the full story. And all of them were prohibited from discussing what they were told. So the fact that they were informed under these extraordinary circumstances does not constitute congressional oversight, and it most certainly does not constitute congressional approval of the program. Indeed, it doesn't even comply with the National Security Act, which requires the entire memberships of the House and Senate Intelligence Committee to be "fully and currently informed of the intelligence activities of the United States."

In addition, we now know that some of these members expressed concern about the program. The Administration ignored their protests. [In early February 2006], one of the eight members of Congress who has been briefed about the program, Congresswoman Jane Harman, ranking member of the House Intelligence Committee, said she sees no reason why the Administration cannot accomplish its goals within the law as currently written.

None of the President's arguments explains or excuses his conduct, or the NSA's domestic spying program. Not one. It is hard to believe that the President has the audacity to claim that they do. It is a strategy that really hinges on the credibility of the office of the Presidency itself. If you just insist that

1. Senate and House leaders Nancy Pelosi, John Boehner, Harry Reida, Mitch McConnell, Silvestre Reyes, Peter Hoekstra, John D. Rockefeller IV, and Kit Bond.

you didn't break the law, you haven't broken the law. It reminds me of what Richard Nixon said after he had left office: "Well, when the president does it that means that it is not illegal." But that is not how our constitutional democracy works. Making those kinds of arguments is damaging the credibility of the Presidency.

And what's particularly disturbing is how many members of Congress have responded. They stood up and cheered. They stood up and cheered.

Justice Louis Brandeis once wrote: "Experience should teach us to be most on our guard to protect liberty when the Government's purposes are beneficent. Men born to freedom are naturally alert to repel invasion of their liberty by evil-minded rulers. The greatest dangers to liberty lurk in insidious encroachment by men of zeal, well-meaning but without understanding."

The President's actions are indefensible. Freedom is an enduring principle. It is not something to celebrate in one breath, and ignore the next. Freedom is at the heart of who we are as a nation, and as a people. We cannot be a beacon of freedom for the world unless we protect our own freedoms here at home.

| *"The Patriot Act has been successful in helping prevent acts of terrorism."*

The Patriot Act Is Helping Prevent Terrorism

Alberto R. Gonzales

Alberto R. Gonzales was sworn in as U.S attorney general in February 2005. In the following viewpoint, Gonzales insists that a set of laws known as the USA Patriot Act of 2001 has been useful in preventing terrorism. He affirms that the act has provided antiterrorist agencies in the United States with increased investigative and surveillance powers to nab suspected terrorists. He also contends that the law has helped these agencies share information so that they can form a more rapid response to terrorist threats. For these reasons, Gonzales urged Congress to renew the act when its provisions were set to expire. Congress did so in March 2006, a few months after this viewpoint was written. Only two of the Patriot Act's provisions were not made permanent during its renewal; one of these, the executive authority to conduct warrantless "roving" wiretaps, is set to expire in 2010.

Alberto R. Gonzales, "Reauthorize the Patriot Act: Congress Should Reauthorize the Patriot Act and Further Strengthen Homeland Security," *Washington Post*, December 14, 2005, p. A29.

As you read, consider the following questions:

1. What are the ways in which the Patriot Act has helped fight terrorism, in Gonzales's view?

2. According to the author, what safeguards to privacy have been added to the Patriot Act since its inception in 2001?

3. What types of oversight does Gonzales say have been used to ensure the Patriot Act is not rushed into renewal?

On Sept. 11, 2001, terrorists inspired by hatred murdered nearly 3,000 innocent Americans. In response, Congress overwhelmingly passed the USA Patriot Act. Now, before it adjourns for the year [in December 2005], Congress must act again to reauthorize this critical piece of legislation. Al Qaeda and other terrorist organizations are at work: Their stated goal is to kill Americans, cripple our economy and demoralize our people.

The bill to be considered . . . is a good one. It equips law enforcement with the tools needed to fight terrorists, and it also includes new civil liberties protections. Members of Congress should put aside the rhetoric and focus on the facts surrounding this vital legislation.

The Patriot Act Works

The Patriot Act has been successful in helping prevent acts of terrorism in many ways. First, it updated anti-terrorism and criminal laws to reflect evolving technologies. Second, it increased penalties for those who commit terrorist crimes. Third, it gave terrorism investigators the same tools used by those who pursue drug dealers and the Mafia. Most important, the act helped break down the wall preventing regular exchange of information between the law enforcement and intelligence communities.

Years later, after a lengthy and extensive public debate, Congress has produced a comprehensive reauthorization bill to permanently reauthorize 14 of the act's 16 expiring provisions. During this important debate, Republicans and Democrats have discovered that concerns raised about the act's impact on civil liberties, while sincere, were unfounded. There have been no verified civil liberties abuses in the four years of the act's existence.

Furthermore, the new bill adds 30 safeguards to protect privacy and civil liberties. Specifically, it includes measures providing that those who receive national security letters may consult an attorney and challenge the request in court; requires high-level Justice Department sign-off before investigators may ask a court to order production of certain sensitive records, such as those from a library; and requires that the FBI describe the target of a "roving wiretap" with sufficient specificity to ensure that only a single individual is targeted.

In addition, this bill further strengthens homeland security by creating a new national security division at the Justice Department, providing additional protections against the threat of attacks on mass transportation systems and at our seaports, and granting us additional tools to protect Americans from terrorism.

Risking U.S. Prevention Efforts

Congress must act now or risk bringing terrorism prevention to a halt. For example, it is widely accepted—and documented by independent bodies such as the Sept. 11 and WMD [weapons of mass destruction] commissions—that a lack of information-sharing and coordination in our government before the attacks of Sept. 11 compromised our ability to connect the dots about what our enemies were doing. The Patriot Act helped dismantle this barrier. And if we allow certain provisions to "sunset" on Jan. 1, we risk shutting down essential intelligence-sharing that occurs in the National Counterterror-

What the Patriot Act Has Accomplished

[Since October 2001] America's law enforcement and intelligence personnel have proved that the Patriot Act works, that it was an important piece of legislation. Since September the 11th, federal terrorism investigations have resulted in charges against more than 400 suspects, and more than half of those charged have been convicted. Federal, state, and local law enforcement have used the Patriot Act to break up terror cells in New York and Oregon and Virginia and in Florida. We've prosecuted terrorist operatives and supporters in California, in Texas, in New Jersey, in Illinois, and North Carolina and Ohio. These efforts have not always made the headlines, but they've made communities safer. The Patriot Act has accomplished exactly what it was designed to do—it has protected American liberty, and saved American lives.

George W. Bush, "President Discusses Patriot Act," June 2005.

ism Center and other facilities where law enforcement officials sit side-by-side with intelligence professionals.

Those who voice concern that Congress is rushing to reauthorize the expiring provisions fail to recognize the oversight it has conducted. In 2005, Congress held 23 hearings focused on reauthorization and heard from more than 60 witnesses. The Justice Department was pleased to provide witnesses at 18 of those hearings, with more than 30 appearances by our experts. I testified three times, explaining the importance of the act, responding to concerns and directly addressing the act's critics. My testimony was informed not only by the successes of the act but also by my personal meetings with representatives from groups such as the ACLU [American Civil Liberties Union] and the American Library Association. During the reauthorization discussion, I asked that certain provisions be clarified to ensure the protection of civil liberties, and Congress responded.

For example, Section 215 of the act permits the government to obtain records on an order issued by a federal judge. I agreed that the statute should allow a recipient of such an order to consult a lawyer and challenge it in court. Further, I agreed that Congress should make explicit the standard under which such orders are issued: relevance to an authorized national security investigation. In 2001 one prominent Democratic senator agreed that the "FBI has made a clear case that a relevance standard is appropriate for counterintelligence and counterterrorism investigations, as well as for criminal investigations."

The president has said that our number-one priority is preventing another catastrophic terrorist attack. Congress must act immediately and reauthorize the Patriot Act before the men and women in law enforcement lose the tools they need to keep us safe.

> "The American people are beginning to realize that this piece of legislation poses a threat to our God-given freedoms protected by the U.S. Constitution."

The Patriot Act Abuses Civil Liberties

John F. McManus

In the following viewpoint, John F. McManus claims that the USA Patriot Act, which was passed in response to the September 11, 2001, attacks on the United States, gives the president authority and powers that are not limited to the pursuit of terrorists. McManus warns that the act licenses snooping on U.S. citizens, including the seizure of business records, the collecting of e-mails, and the wiretapping of phone calls. He sees these executive powers as evidence of "empire building," not respect for the Constitution and the constraints of the presidential office. McManus suggests that Congress limit these powers as the Patriot Act comes up for renewal. Within a month of the printing of McManus's views, however, Congress chose to extend the majority of the privileges granted by the act. John F. McManus is president of the John Birch Society, an organization dedicated to preserving individual liberty.

John F. McManus, "The Patriot Act: Bad Medicine," *New American*, vol. 22, no. 2, January 23, 2006. Copyright © 2006 American Opinion Publishing Incorporated. Reproduced by permission.

As you read, consider the following questions:

1. What evidence does McManus give for claiming that the Patriot Act was initially rushed through Congress?
2. According to the author, why does President George W. Bush believe the Patriot Act needs to be renewed?

It's one thing to add a spoonful of sugar to make the medicine go down. But it's quite another to go to enormous lengths to convince a patient that the medicine itself is the sugar. Yet this is substantially what the [George W.] Bush administration and its allies in the building of an imperial presidency did when they labeled their grasp for power "The Patriot Act."

The act's full name is "Uniting and Strengthening America by Providing Appropriate Tools Required to Intercept and Obstruct Terrorism Act of 2001." Rushed through Congress in the aftermath of the 9/11 terrorist attacks, it has long been touted as a necessary tool to prevent more attacks. Containing over 500 pages of detailed and lawyer-like verbiage, it is certain that no member had an opportunity to study it before being asked to approve it.

Unchecked Snooping

While no one can doubt that the federal government should have responded to the 9/11 treachery, the American people are beginning to realize that this piece of legislation poses a threat to our God-given freedoms protected by the U.S. Constitution. For instance, the act increases the ability of law enforcement to search homes and business records secretly; it expands wiretapping and surveillance authority; and it creates an entirely new mechanism for obtaining proper search warrants and then engaging in electronic snooping of email, telephone calls, and internet messaging. Under its provisions, persons ordered to turn over business records are not permitted to contact an attorney or seek the protection of the courts.

Further, its provisions are far from clearly stated, giving almost free rein to federal officials to use the act and then rely on the courts to uphold the legitimacy of what they have done.

Those who wrote the act expected resistance to its sweeping grants of power, so they added a "sunset" provision stipulating that some of its surveillance powers "shall cease to have effect on December 31, 2005." President Bush wants the entire act extended but many in Congress, buttressed with years to study it and learn of its dangers to liberty, have seen enough and want to bury its extremely controversial portions. So, the compromisers took over. Prior to the December 31 expiration date Congress voted to extend the sunset provision five weeks, to February 3. On that date, some of the most intrusive surveillance powers in the bill—such as using "roving" wiretaps, searching property without notifying its owner, and scrutinizing business records, books, and other documents—will die, unless those powers are again extended or (as the president wants) are made permanent.

No Extensions

What's at stake here are provisions of the Bill of Rights. Do we or do we not have the Fourth Amendment's guarantee that all Americans shall "be secure in their persons, houses, papers, and effects against unreasonable searches and seizure"? Do we or don't we have assurance that such a God-given right "shall not be violated" without a warrant demonstrating "probable cause, supported by Oath of affirmation, and particularly describing the place to be searched, and the person or things to be seized"? Provisions of the Patriot Act now set to expire effectively cancel this essential guarantee.

President Bush has repeatedly insisted that all of the Patriot Act is needed because "we're still at war," a war he boastfully claims was launched on "my decision" and nobody else's. His disdain for the constitutional requirement that only Congress can send the nation into war, and his desire to trash the 4th Amendment, are indications of empire building, not limited government under the Constitution.

These developments surely threaten the preservation of freedom that has long characterized our nation's hard-won republic. No matter what Mr. Bush may claim, the main issue here isn't the protection of the American people from terrorism. Doing so can be accomplished without trampling on the Constitution. The issue is whether our national government will be properly limited or become all powerful.

Ominously growing presidential power must be reined in. An increasingly docile Congress can begin the needed process by refusing to extend the Patriot Act's most dangerous surveillance powers. Blocking their renewal will send a message to the president and his administration that they possess only limited powers and do not have a blank check to build an empire.

Periodical Bibliography

The following articles have been selected to supplement the diverse views presented in this chapter.

David Cole	"Patriot Act Post-mortem," *Nation*, April 3, 2006.
Stephen Handelman	"Technology vs. Terrorism," *Popular Science*, September 2006.
Shane Harris	"Terrorist Profiling, Version 2.0," *National Journal*, October 21, 2006.
Terence P. Jeffrey	"Establish Terrorist Defense Initiative to Keep Americans Safe," *Human Events*, January 29, 2007.
William Kristol and Gary Schmitt	"Vital Presidential Power," *Washington Post*, December 20, 2005.
Eric Lichtblau and Mark Mazzetti	"Military Expands Intelligence Role in U.S.," *New York Times*, January 14, 2007.
Nation	"The Insecurity State," June 5, 2006.
National Review	"Misplaced Fears," June 5, 2006.
Andrew Potter	"If Security Fails, There Is Always a Scapegoat: Freedom," *Maclean's*, September 11, 2006.
Rosemary Radford Ruether	"In the Name of Security," *National Catholic Reporter*, June 16, 2006.
Jonathan Weisman	"GOP Leaders Back Bush on Wiretapping, Tribunals," *Washington Post*, September 14, 2006.
Armstrong Williams	"If You're Not a Terrorist, Don't Worry," *New York Amsterdam News*, February 9, 2006.
Mortimer B. Zuckerman	"Let's Use All the Tools," *U.S. News & World Report*, May 29, 2006.

OPPOSING
VIEWPOINTS®
SERIES

CHAPTER 4

How Can U.S. National Security Be Improved?

Chapter Preface

Terrorism consultant Alexis Debat and *National Interest* editor Nikolas K. Gvosdev wrote an article in the September/October 2006 issue of that magazine that charged America with being too vulnerable to terrorist threats. According to the authors, the U.S. government is partitioned, not unified, so centralizing command and intelligence is a difficult task. Divisions in the political arena also reveal that the nation is not clear on how best to respond to terrorism, Debat and Gvosdev argue, nor is the government able to create a long-term consensual strategy with politicians changing guard every two or four years. The pair also blames American society as a whole for putting too much faith in "providence" for protection instead of making sacrifices in the name of security. "America, not only its politicians but also its people, will have to make hard choices, and decide now what it will and will not do in the pursuit of security against the terrorist threat," Debat and Gvosdev conclude.

James Fallows, a national correspondent for the *Atlantic*, is less pessimistic about the nation's security—especially from terrorist attacks from organizations like al Qaeda. After interviewing military, intelligence, business, and academic leaders, Fallows found that most believed al Qaeda was no longer a serious threat—at least in terms of its ability to wage a successful terrorism campaign on the scale of the September 11, 2001, tragedy. According to those interviewed, the U.S. military has delivered crippling blows to al Qaeda's organization and leadership and deprived it of its training bases. The U.S. government, in conjunction with other world governments, has also dried up al Qaeda's funds and made connections to the organization a disadvantage for any nation wishing to take part in the global economy. Although Fallows agrees that al Qaeda is still a thorn in America's side that needs to be watched vigilantly, he maintains that "its hopes for fundamentally harming the United States now rest less on what it can do itself than on what it can trick, tempt, or goad us into doing. Its destiny is no longer in its own hands." Fallows suggests that America's leadership declare victory and end the war on terror. He warns that by keeping the nation on a war footing, the government fuels hysteria that leads to curtailments of civil liberties and other disproportionate reactions to an overblown threat. And that, he insists, only serves to aid terrorism's objectives.

In the following chapter, analysts and commentators debate how America can best respond to national security threats in the age of terrorism and weapons of mass destruction. Some believe that the United States needs to increase its arsenal and become more mindful of the openness of its society; others caution that too much safeguarding can deprive the nation of the very liberties on which it was founded.

"We live in a dangerous world, and there is no excuse for our government to fail to build the best defenses we can in order to save American lives."

The United States Needs a Missile Defense

Phyllis Schlafly

Phyllis Schlafly argues in the following viewpoint that the United States needs a ballistic missile defense. Schlafly argues that because of imminent threats from rogue nations—like North Korea—that are seeking nuclear capabilities, the government cannot be assured that unstable regimes will not launch missile attacks against the United States or its allies. In addition, she suggests that the possession of a missile defense may deter foreign powers from even seeking nuclear weapons. Phyllis Schlafly is a noted conservative columnist and founder of the Eagle Forum, a conservative organization concerned with social issues, family values, and public policy.

As you read, consider the following questions:

1. As Schlafly notes, what does *SDI* stand for and with which U.S. president was it first associated?

Phyllis Schlafly, "President Reagan Was Right on Missile Defense," *Human Events*, vol. 62, no. 24, July 17, 2006, pp. 1–5. Copyright 2006 Human Events Inc. Reproduced by permission.

2. According to the author, what two arguments do liberals use to oppose the creation of a missile defense system?

3. As Schlafly states, what is the "best way to discourage nuclear proliferation?"

North Korea's threat to test a long-range missile capable of reaching the United States comes as no surprise. President George W. Bush already branded North Korea as part of the "axis of evil."

This North Korean threat dramatically confirms the need for the anti-missile defense system that President Ronald Reagan called for in his famous nationally televised address of March 23, 1983. At the time Reagan made that landmark speech, our national strategy for dealing with the Soviet nuclear threat was called Mutual Assured Destruction, known by its acronym MAD.

The Ability to Save Lives

Reagan and most conservatives (including the editors of *Human Events*), believed it was, indeed, MAD to continue with a plan that simply threatened the Russians that if they bombed the United States, we would bomb them back and kill millions of Russians. We had no Plan B.

Reagan exposed the fallacy in MAD when he posed the crucial question, "Would it not be better to save lives than to avenge them?" Reagan had no qualms about criticizing the mistaken policies of his predecessors.

Sen. Edward M. Kennedy (D-Mass.) and the anti-defense claque (chanting on cue like a Greek chorus) ridiculed Reagan's plan as Star Wars, but Reagan's vision was accurate and his goal was and is essential. That was the start of our anti-ballistic missile defense, known as the Strategic Defense Initiative, or SDI.

We now know that Reagan's determination to build a U.S. antimissile system, which he staunchly defended at summits in

Toward a Global Missile Defense

Other countries, including Italy, Britain, India, Australia, Canada, Greenland, Denmark, Poland, and Israel, are already developing missile defense systems that would integrate into American systems. In September 2002 statements by Russian deputy foreign and defense ministers revealed a willingness to cooperate with Washington on 'GMD' [Global Missile Defense]. One realizes that the Kremlin is keen to promote and protect this potentially profit-making element of its defense sector. The US has already offered outright an 'umbrella' effect that a 'GMD' could have that would protect other countries.

Kevin Roeten, "There Is NO Alternative to Missile Defense,"
American Daily, *November 25, 2006. Reproduced by permission.*

Geneva [Switzerland] and Reykjavik [Iceland], was the fundamental reason he won the Cold War without firing a shot. [Former president of the Soviet Union] Mikhail Gorbachev realized the Soviets could not compete with the United States, and that started the collapse of the Soviet empire.

Delays and Opposition

For nearly 30 years, the United States was handicapped from going forward with Reagan's SDI by the 1972 Anti-Ballistic Missile Treaty [ABM] that had been so foolishly negotiated by [former secretary of state] Henry Kissinger and signed by President Richard M. Nixon. If we had had a Supreme Court as eager to cut back on presidential power as we had in the recent Hamdan case,[1] the ABM treaty could have been ruled unconstitutional because it violated our government's constitutional duty to "provide for the common defense."

1. In June 2006, the U.S. Supreme Court ruled that a Yemeni detainee (Salin Ahmed Hamdan) could not be tried by a military tribunal as the administration of President George W. Bush intended.

President Bush understood this and, in one of his most important acts, in December 2001 he withdrew from the ABM Treaty. Bush ignored noisy objections from Russian President Vladimir Putin.

Liberals have nevertheless kept up their opposition to deploying an effective ABM defense. They pretend to be worried about the cost (although they are never deterred by the high cost of government programs they like), and budget requests for missile defense funds were cut in half during the administrations of President Bill Clinton. The liberals' other argument is that an ABM system won't work. We need the American can-do attitude expressed in a popular World War II slogan: "The difficult we do today; the impossible may take a little longer."

Proliferation Problems

The Bush Administration has moved steadily to build several methods of defense against both short-range and long-range missiles and many tests have been successful. However, we still have no capability of destroying an ICBM [intercontinental ballistic missile] in its boost phase.

A functioning ABM system might be even more necessary in the post–September 11 world than in Reagan's world. In 1983, the terrible nukes could be built only by superpowers with a sophisticated technological base. Today we are in an era of rogue nations with irrational dictators and poor man's missiles that can be built and launched relatively inexpensively, and might even be bought from cash-hungry Russians who still have 3,500 long-range missiles and up to 15,000 smaller tactical nuclear weapons.

In addition to facing down intimidation from North Korea and Iran, the United States needs anti-missile defenses because China is using the huge amounts of cash it gets from U.S. trade to modernize its ballistic missile arsenal.

We live in a dangerous world, and there is no excuse for our government to fail to build the best defenses we can in order to save American lives.

If we shoot down a North Korean missile with our own anti-missile system, that would send a powerful message to North Korea that its tactics are a loser. It would also reassure Japan and other U.S. allies that we have the will to protect them from rogue madmen.

The best way to discourage nuclear proliferation would be to demonstrate that the United States is willing and able to destroy their missiles before they hit their targets. It's time for the United States to let the world know that we have an anti-ballistic missile defense system to protect our people and our allies, and that we will use it.

| "Star Wars [missile defense system] ...
is a military choice, not a necessity."

The United States Does Not Need a Missile Defense

Nuclear Age Peace Foundation

Established in 1982, the Nuclear Age Peace Foundation is a global organization dedicated to abolishing nuclear weapons and finding peaceful solutions to international crises. In the following viewpoint, the foundation argues that the United States does not need a missile defense system to intercept nuclear attacks. Such a system is unproven and extremely costly, the organization contends. The Nuclear Age Peace Foundation asserts that the money earmarked for missile defense would be better spent improving civic infrastructure and providing for the health and education needs of Americans.

As you read, consider the following questions:

1. How does the Nuclear Age Peace Foundation dismiss the potential threats from North Korea, Iran, China, and al Qaeda?

Nuclear Age Peace Foundation, "Is Missile Defense Really Needed?" *San Francisco Chronicle*, May 23, 2004. Republished with permission of *San Francisco Chronicle*, conveyed through Copyright Clearance Center, Inc.

2. According to the author, on what did forty-nine retired senior military officers say the money for missile defense could be better spent?

3. What was entailed in former secretary of defense Donald Rumsfeld's "Vision 2020" report that is of concern to the Nuclear Age Peace Foundation?

President Ronald Reagan had a dream. Let's build a missile shield that will protect us from our enemy's nuclear missiles. In popular culture, we called it Star Wars and ever since, our country has been spending billions of dollars to try to create an anti-ballistic missile system.

Now, the [George W.] Bush administration plans to deploy a national missile defense system in California and Alaska that has already cost $130 billion. [In 2004], the Bush budget call[ed] for spending yet another $10.2 billion.

But who is the enemy? If it's North Korea, diplomatic reassurance that we will not invade that country will work better than a still unproven missile system. If it's China, why have we given them "most-favored nation" trade status? If it's Iran, they do not have the nuclear material or the missiles with which to attack the United States. If it's [the terrorist group] al Qaeda, no missile shield will protect us from a dirty bomb, the dispersion of biological or chemical weapons or suicide bombers who decide to detonate themselves in our shopping malls.

Nothing for the Money

But the real problem with the missile shield is that scientists say there is virtually no proof that we Americans have gotten anything for our billions of dollars. Nevertheless, President Bush is determined to get Star Wars up and running.... Why? Probably because he wants to prove that, despite the disarray and scandal in Iraq, he is the leader who can protect our national security.

Missile Defense Makes No Sense

If America continues down the current path of trying to field a viable missile-defense system, significant cuts will need to be made in other areas of the defense budget, or funds reallocated from other nonmilitary spending programs. With America already engaged in a costly war in Iraq, and with the possibility of additional conflict with Iran, Syria, or North Korea looming on the horizon, funding a missile-defense system that not only does not work as designed, but even if it did, would not be capable of defending America from threats such as the [sophisticated Russian] Topol-M missile, makes no sense.

Scott Ritter, "Rude Awakening to Missile-Defense Dream,"
Christian Science Monitor, *January 4, 2005.*
Reproduced by permission.

Scientists, however, have voiced great doubt that any part of Star Wars can work. In a May [2004], 76-page report titled "Technical Realities," the Union of Concerned Scientists found "no basis for believing the system will have any capability to defend against a real attack."

In addition, 49 retired senior military officers, including a former chairman of the Joint Chiefs of Staff, wrote an "Open Letter to the President" in March [2004], asking Bush to postpone deployment of an untested and unproven ground-based missile shield. Instead, they want the president to use these billions to "accelerate programs to secure the multitude of facilities containing nuclear weapons and materials and to protect our ports and borders against terrorists who may attempt to smuggle weapons of mass destruction into the United States."

They have asked Bush to commit these billions of dollars to fortifying our nation's seaports and trains and other sites vulnerable to terrorists.

Where Missile Defense Money Could Go

In addition to improving homeland security, think what California's share of these billions could buy. Money that's projected for ballistic missile defense . . . , for example, could pay for 205,234 housing vouchers or health care for 413,584 uninsured adults or 21,569 elementary school teachers, or 6,079 fire engines, or 163,534 Head Start placements or health care for 949,480 children.

Beyond spending precious taxpayer dollars, Star Wars has voided the 1972 Anti-Ballistic Missile treaty and is likely to ignite an arms race with other countries—perhaps China.

Nor is the missile shield completely defensive. As many critics have noted, the technology needed to make a ballistic-missile system work perfectly also creates the ability to build offensive space-based weapons, which would violate the Outer Space Treaty of 1967.

Late in the fall of 2001, [former] Secretary of Defense Donald Rumsfeld delivered to Congress a report from a task force he chaired. It was called "Vision 2020" and described how the United States could use space-based weapons to dominate the world. Such military dominance, however, will only intensify fear and resentment of our nation and likely result in even more terrorist attacks. Memo to the President: You can't win an urban battle in Fallujah [Iraq] with space-based weapons.

Star Wars, like the war in Iraq, is a military choice, not a necessity. We don't need more weapons to secure our future. What we need are solutions to the ethnic and religious clashes and political and economic inequities that divide the people on this planet.

| "In an era where there is justifiable fear
of terrorism, a national ID card would
also help law enforcement."

National ID Cards Would
Make America Safer

James Sensenbrenner (Part I) and Robert Kuttner (Part II)

In 2005, U.S. representative from Wisconsin James Sensenbrenner backed an initiative for the states to implement a new driver's license program to increase national security. In part I of the following viewpoint, Sensenbrenner explains why his Real ID Act would help America keep accurate records of drivers and prevent foreign visitors from obtaining licenses and other important documents that could aid them in carrying out terrorism. The Real ID Act became law in May 2005. In part II of the viewpoint, Robert Kuttner, coeditor of the American Prospect *magazine, states that he is in favor of the implementation of a national ID card. According to Kuttner, such a card could benefit voter registration, help handle immigration issues, and aid law enforcement in the age of terrorism.*

Part I: James Sensenbrenner, "Plan Would Protect U.S.," *USA Today*, May 10, 2005.
Part II: Robert Kuttner, "Try National ID Card—You Might Like It," *Boston Globe*, December 8, 2004. Reproduced by permission of the author.

As you read, consider the following questions:

1. According to Sensenbrenner, how might the Real ID card have stopped the September 11 terrorists from carrying out their plan?
2. In what way would a national ID card benefit voter registration, in Kuttner's opinion?
3. What kinds of laws must be tightened, in Kuttner's view, for citizens to accept a national ID card?

Part I

On Sept. 11, 2001, 18 of the 19 hijackers deliberately used valid driver's licenses and state ID's—as opposed to their passports—as their document of choice to board the airplanes. Why? Because state IDs allowed the hijackers to avoid suspicion. A driver's license allows freedom of movement and conveys credibility.

Noting that "for terrorists, travel documents are as important as weapons," the 9/11 Commission recommended the federal government set national standards for the issuance of driver's licenses and stated, "Fraud in identification documents is no longer just a problem of theft."

The Real ID Act would ensure states have strict security standards when they issue driver's licenses and ID cards if their citizens want them to be accepted as identification for boarding an airplane, entering a nuclear power plant or interacting with the federal government. Lax standards by a few states put all Americans at risk.

Real ID would require all states to confirm the identities of applicants, confirm that visas are valid for foreign visitors, keep accurate records, and make driver's licenses and ID cards extremely difficult to counterfeit. This legislation would prevent the next [September 11 terrorist hijacker] Mohammed Atta from using his six-month visa to obtain a six-year driver's license by requiring that a foreign visitor's license term ends when the visa expires. Furthermore, once these reforms are in place with more complete state records, license renewals should be faster and lines shorter.

Real ID is estimated to cost the average state less than $2 million to comply with over five years, a small price for closing a large security loophole. It would authorize federal grants to help share states' costs.

This legislation would not create a national ID card or a national database. Rather, it would require states to improve the data security of the information they already hold and build upon the current interaction of the different states' motor vehicle departments.

While we did not prevent 9/11 from happening, the Real ID Act is vital to preventing foreign terrorists from hiding in plain sight while planning another attack just like it.

Part II

As a card-carrying member of the American Civil Liberties Union, I'd like to have one more card in my wallet. The card I want, contrary to the views of most civil liberties activists, is a national ID card.

Privacy advocates have always resisted this idea, for fear of government snooping on citizens. But that cat is out of the bag. Nearly all of us have driver's licenses, Social Security cards, passports. And corporations, credit agencies, and HMOs [health maintenance organizations] keep dossiers, too—often more extensive than what government maintains.

For civil libertarians, the real issue is not whether government and business collect databases on citizens, but whether there are adequate protections against abuses.

Those protections have come under particular assault in the era of George W. Bush and the USA Patriot Act. But we will not solve the privacy problem by pretending that we are back in a pre-computer era. For that matter, Hitler did not need computers to abuse citizens.

Minimum Document Requirements of the Real ID Law

To meet the requirements of this section, a State shall include, at a minimum, the following information and features on each driver's license and identification card issued to a person by the State:

1. The person's full legal name.
2. The person's date of birth.
3. The person's gender.
4. The person's driver's license or identification card number.
5. A digital photograph of the person.
6. The person's address of principal residence.
7. The person's signature.
8. Physical security features designed to prevent tampering, counterfeiting, or duplication of the document for fraudulent purposes.
9. A common machine-readable technology, with defined minimum data elements.

In general—to meet the requirements of this section, a State shall require, at a minimum, presentation and verification of the following information. . .

1. A photo identity document, except that a nonphoto identity document is acceptable if it includes both the person's full legal name and date of birth.
2. Documentation showing the person's date of birth.
3. Proof of the person's social security account number or verification that the person is not eligible for a social security account number.
4. Documentation showing the person's name and address of principal residence.

119 Stat. 231 Public Law 109-13—May 11, 2005.
http://frwebgate.access.gpo.gov.

Voter Registration and Immigration Rights

There are several good reasons to support a national ID card. The first has to do with voter registration and democracy.

Tens of millions of Americans don't vote because we make voters go through a two-step process of registering and then voting. As we saw in the elections of 2000 and 2004, the registration process is an invitation to endless political mischief.

In fact, registration was introduced in the late 19th century precisely to hold down the numbers of votes from former slaves and from recent immigrants. It still functions to hold down voting today.

In most countries, the national ID card certifies your identity, age, and citizenship. That's it. You present the card, and you vote.

In America, millions of volunteer hours and hundreds of millions of dollars go into the needless process of registering voters—time and money that could go toward political activism and education. So a national ID card, with proper safeguards, would make America more democratic, not less.

The second big reason involves immigration and labor rights. We try to control our borders, but millions of foreigners overstay tourist or student visas or slip in illegally, in order to work. They are able to take jobs because business wants them here to work for low wages and be conveniently frightened of exercising their labor rights.

Our immigration laws require workers to have proof of lawful status, but employers are not punished if the papers turn out to be forgeries, which are easy to obtain. It's much harder to forge a passport-quality national ID card.

So let's decide just what level of immigration we want, make it possible for those immigrants currently working in the country to regularize their status, and then use a national ID card to make clear who is able to work—and to freely exercise rights as workers without fear of being deported.

Helping Law Enforcement

In an era where there is justifiable fear of terrorism, a national ID card would also help law enforcement. Identity theft would also be much harder if there were a single, government issued ID card.

A national ID card could help government pursue valuable record keeping, for instance to make sure that all children are immunized, and to pursue epidemiological research that is now difficult or impossible. A single government ID card would dramatically reduce underage drinking. Frail elderly people would cease having to renew drivers licenses solely for the purpose of ID. But libertarians are absolutely right to worry about potential and actual abuses. So the other side of the bargain is a much tougher set of laws protecting against improper invasions of privacy and snooping, both by government and by corporations.

There should be tougher penalties if an HMO sells confidential medical records. We need stronger measures against unwanted telemarketing, and against abuse of credit records.

The so-called USA Patriot Act has outrageous provisions, such as warrant-less snooping and "sneak and peek" searches in which the subject of the search is never informed that his or her privacy has been violated. These need to be repealed and replaced with far narrower search and seizure provisions that are not broad fishing licenses.

Right now, we liberty-loving Americans have the worst of both worlds. Far too many databases keep far too much information on us, with too few controls on its misuse. Yet we don't take advantage of the most basic uses of ID, such as making clear who is properly in the country and making it easier for citizens to vote.

> *"Once it is put in place, a national ID card program will actually make us less secure."*

National ID Cards Would Not Make America Safer

Bruce Schneier

In the following viewpoint, security technologist and author Bruce Schneier argues that a national ID card would not protect Americans from terrorism or other criminal acts. Schneier maintains that criminals would learn how to forge these cards or would provide false names to acquire them. He also states that such cards would necessitate the creation of a database filled with personal information and that this database would be a vulnerable target of hackers and others who could gain from identity theft.

As you read, consider the following questions:

1. Why does the fact that many people will honestly lose ID cards jeopardize the program, in Schneier's view?
2. According to the author, what problem might occur if the ID database were struck with a virus?

Bruce Schneier, "A National ID Card Wouldn't Make Us Safer," *Minneapolis Star Tribune*, April 1, 2004. Copyright Cowles Media Co. 2004. Reproduced with permission of *Star Tribune*, Minneapolis-St. Paul.

3. Why does Schneier think that a national ID would not have stopped Oklahoma City bomber Timothy McVeigh or other terrorists?

As a security technologist, I regularly encounter people who say the United States should adopt a national ID card. How could such a program not make us more secure, they ask?

The suggestion, when it's made by a thoughtful civic-minded person like [*New York Times* columnist] Nicholas Kristof, . . . often takes on a tone that is regretful and ambivalent: Yes, indeed, the card would be a minor invasion of our privacy, and undoubtedly it would add to the growing list of interruptions and delays we encounter every day, but we live in dangerous times, we live in a new world. . . .

It all sounds so reasonable, but there's a lot to disagree with in such an attitude.

National IDs Will Not Make Americans Secure

The potential privacy encroachments of an ID card system are far from minor. And the interruptions and delays caused by incessant ID checks could easily proliferate into a persistent traffic jam in office lobbies and airports and hospital waiting rooms and shopping malls.

But my primary objection isn't the totalitarian potential of national IDs, nor the likelihood that they'll create a whole immense new class of social and economic dislocations. Nor is it the opportunities they will create for colossal boondoggles by government contractors. My objection to the national ID card, at least for the purposes of this essay, is much simpler.

It won't work. It won't make us more secure.

In fact, everything I've learned about security over the last 20 years tells me that once it is put in place, a national ID card program will actually make us less secure.

My argument may not be obvious, but it's not hard to follow, either. It centers around the notion that security must be evaluated not based on how it works, but on how it fails.

It doesn't really matter how well an ID card works when used by the hundreds of millions of honest people that would carry it. What matters is how the system might fail when used by someone intent on subverting that system: how it fails naturally, how it can be made to fail, and how failures might be exploited.

Forgery and Fraud Problems

The first problem is the card itself. No matter how unforgeable we make it, it will be forged. And even worse, people will get legitimate cards in fraudulent names.

Two of the 9/11 terrorists had valid Virginia driver's licenses in fake names. And even if we could guarantee that everyone who issued national ID cards couldn't be bribed, initial cardholder identity would be determined by other identity documents . . . all of which would be easier to forge.

Not that there would ever be such a thing as a single ID card. Currently about 20 percent of all identity documents are lost per year. An entirely separate security system would have to be developed for people who lost their card, a system that itself is capable of abuse.

Additionally, any ID system involves people—people who regularly make mistakes. We all have stories of bartenders falling for obviously fake IDs, or sloppy ID checks at airports and government buildings. It's not simply a matter of training: checking IDs is a mind-numbingly boring task, one that is guaranteed to have failures. Biometrics such as thumbprints show some promise here but bring with them their own set of exploitable failure modes.

Database Vulnerability

But the main problem with any ID system is that it requires the existence of a database. In this case it would have to be an immense database of private and sensitive information on every American—one widely and instantaneously accessible from airline check-in stations, police cars, schools, and so on.

The security risks are enormous. Such a database would be a kludge of existing databases; databases that are incompatible, full of erroneous data, and unreliable. As computer scientists, we do not know how to keep a database of this magnitude secure, whether from outside hackers or the thousands of insiders authorized to access it.

And when the inevitable worms, viruses, or random failures happen and the database goes down, what then? Is America supposed to shut down until it's restored?

Proponents of national ID cards want us to assume all these problems, and the tens of billions of dollars such a system would cost—for what? For the promise of being able to identify someone?

What good would it have been to know the names of Timothy McVeigh, the Unabomber, or the DC snipers before they were arrested? Palestinian suicide bombers generally have no history of terrorism. The goal here is to know someone's intentions, and their identity has very little to do with that.

And there are security benefits in having a variety of different ID documents. A single national ID is an exceedingly valuable document, and accordingly there's greater incentive to forge it. There is more security in alert guards paying attention to subtle social cues than bored minimum-wage guards blindly checking IDs.

That's why, when someone asks me to rate the security of a national ID card on a scale of one to 10, I can't give an answer. It doesn't even belong on a scale.

Periodical Bibliography

The following articles have been selected to supplement the diverse views presented in this chapter.

Jonathan Broder et al.	"Deep Pockets for a 'Long War,'" *CQ Weekly*, March 27, 2006.
Philip E. Coyle	"The Limits and Liabilities of Missile Defense," *Current History*, November 2006.
Frank J. Gaffney Jr.	"U.S. Must Move to Full Missile Defense," *Human Events*, October 9, 2006.
Mark Halpern	"Buggy Software and Missile Defense," *New Atlantis*, Fall 2005.
Marisa Katz	"Novel Approach," *New Republic*, November 6, 2006.
Eric Lipton	"New Detectors Aim to Prevent Nuclear Terror," *New York Times*, February 9, 2007.
Tom Plate	"International Bad Boy Kim Jong Il Should Be Among the Least of Our Worries: U.S. Must Learn to Live with North Korea's Antics," *San Diego Business Journal*, November 6, 2006.
Jacob Sullum	"ID Card Trick," *Reason*, August/September 2005.
USA Today	"Big Brother Is on the Move," December 2005.
Wall Street Journal	"Real Bad ID," October 10, 2006.
Wall Street Journal	"The Taepodong Democrats: Still Against Missile Defense, Even in the Age of Kim Jong Il," July 21, 2006.

For Further Discussion

Chapter 1

1. After reading the viewpoints of Donald H. Rumsfeld and Robert Dreyfuss, explain whether you think terrorism is still a threat to American security or whether it is an overblown fear. Whichever viewpoint you defend, explain why you think opponents would choose to believe and promote the opposite view. Use the arguments of Rumsfeld, Dreyfuss, Mortimer B. Zuckerman, and any other critic or commentator to support your analysis.

2. In 2010 a group of jihadists, funded by sympathetic Middle Eastern oil financiers, purchases weapons-grade plutonium from a stockpile in the former Soviet republics. After fashioning a crude bomb, the extremists transport the device to Central America and then drive it overland through Mexico to smuggle it into the United States. Once inside the border, the group detonates the bomb in a major metropolitan city. Considering the viewpoints of Richard G. Lugar and Ivan Eland, how possible do you think this scenario is? Using the authors' arguments, explain why you think this terrorist act could occur or how it would likely be foiled at any stage.

3. Michael T. Klare and Ron Paul suggest threats to national security that are not of a military or terrorist nature. Do you think these threats are more pressing than terrorism or weapons of mass destruction? Explain why or why not. Can you think of other threats to national security that have not been mentioned in this book? What are they and how do they threaten America's security?

Chapter 2

1. In George W. Bush's view, the United States must stay committed to fighting insurgency in Iraq because a fallen Iraq would become a breeding ground for anti-American terrorists. Do you believe Iraq is now or could become a haven for terrorists? Or do you agree with Brian Katulis, who argues that the longer the United States stays in Iraq, the more likely the civil disruption could destabilize the region and greatly exacerbate anti-American sentiment? In other words, address how important you think the U.S. mission in Iraq is to the War on Terror?

2. According to Mario Loyola, what advantages would the United States have if it had to pursue military action against Iran's nuclear program? In Zbigniew Brzezinski's view, what are the disadvantages of following a military path in contending with Iran? After weighing the pros and cons, what do you think America's policy in Iran should be? Is Iran's nuclear program worth eliminating? If so, how? If not, can the United States tolerate a nuclear Iran, in your opinion? Explain your answers.

3. In October 2006 North Korea declared to the world that it had detonated a nuclear device. American commentators like those represented in this chapter were quick to offer ways to address this supposed threat to global security. After reading the viewpoints, do you think any of the proposed courses of action are the correct ones to pursue in addressing the North Korean threat? Explain which one(s) you favor and why you would reject the other proposals. In February 2007 North Korea agreed to suspend its nuclear program in return for economic privileges and to allow UN inspectors into its nuclear reactor to guarantee its compliance with the bargain. After making this agreement, North Korean officials were reported to have said that the cessation of its nuclear program is only "tempo-

rary." Does this new occurrence change your opinion on what course of action the United States should pursue? Explain.

Chapter 3

1. Critics such as Stephen Flynn maintain that the Department of Homeland Security (DHS) is hampered because other intelligence agencies are often reluctant and not compelled to share information with the relatively new department. The *New York Times* levels more criticisms of the department's lackluster job of securing chemical plants, nuclear reactors, and other potential terrorist targets around the nation. Michael Chertoff, however, recounts important accomplishments of the DHS during his tenure as its secretary. Looking at the evidence presented in both viewpoints, do you think America's homeland is well-protected against terrorist attack? In answering the question, list the country's vulnerabilities that you think need the most attention from the department.

2. After reading the two viewpoints on the National Security Agency (NSA) surveillance program and the pair on the renewal of the Patriot Act, explain whether you believe the War on Terror requires the curtailment or surrendering of some civil liberties. Is the government justified in targeting some or all Americans for surveillance of terrorist connections? If so, what means can ensure that the rights of Americans are not excessively violated? If you do not agree that the government should be spying on its own residents, how can U.S. security be protected? In your estimation of the information provided in the viewpoints, do you think the surveillance programs have been successful in stopping terrorism? Explain your answers.

Chapter 4

1. The Nuclear Age Peace Foundation argues against the implementation of a "Star Wars" defense plan that envisions a space-based missile shield that could be used offensively as well as defensively. The foundation conjectures that such unprecedented power may increase global hostility toward the United States rather than ensure the nation's security. Do you think a missile defense system is needed to protect America from foreign powers that are seeking nuclear weapons, or could such a defensive shield backfire by engendering anti-American sentiment in the world? Furthermore, do you believe the U.S. government might use such a system offensively? Do you think there would be a way to safeguard against this possibility?

2. The Nuclear Age Peace Foundation believes that money that funds unproven and costly defense projects would be better spent on improving domestic welfare programs and developing energy technologies that would wean the country off fossil fuels. Phyllis Schlafly, on the other hand, contends that the United States needs the most up-to-date military weaponry to fend off increasingly sophisticated enemies. After reading both viewpoints, decide whether you think the nation needs to improve its military deterrence or whether America should spend its tax monies in other ways. Explain why you favor one view over the other, and state how you would strike a balance between defense needs and the pressing concerns of social improvement.

3. Explain how you feel about the possible implementation of a national identity card. Do you think mandating a national ID would prove beneficial to Americans or would it be an imposition? Address some of the arguments made by James Sensenbrenner, Robert Kuttner, and Bruce Schneier in framing your answer.

Organizations to Contact

The editors have compiled the following list of organizations concerned with the issues debated in this book. The descriptions are derived from materials provided by the organizations. All have publications or information available for interested readers. The list was compiled on the date of publication of the present volume; the information provided here may change. Be aware that many organizations take several weeks or longer to respond to inquiries, so allow as much time as possible.

American Civil Liberties Union (ACLU)
125 Broad St., 18th Floor, New York, NY   10004-2400
(212) 549-2500
e-mail: aclu@aclu.org
Web site: www.aclu.org

The ACLU is a national organization that champions American civil liberties. The ACLU maintains the position that government expediency and national security should not compromise fundamental civil liberties. The ACLU publishes and distributes policy statements, pamphlets, and press releases with titles such as "In Defense of Freedom in a Time of Crisis" and "National ID Cards: 5 Reasons Why They Should Be Rejected."

American Enterprise Institute (AEI)
1150 Seventeenth St. NW, Washington, DC   20036
(202) 862-5800 • fax: (202) 862-7177
Web site: www.aei.org

AEI is a nonpartisan organization dedicated to preserving limited government, private enterprise, and a strong national defense. The institute's main areas of research include economic policy, social and political studies, and defense and foreign policy. It has issued many articles on terrorism and America's involvement in the Middle East. AEI publishes the bimonthly magazine the *American* and provides many of its publications on its Web site.

The Brookings Institution
1775 Massachusetts Ave. NW, Washington, DC   20036
(202) 797-6000 • fax: (202) 797-6004
e-mail: brookinfo@brook.edu
Web site: www.brookings.edu

The Brookings Institution is a think tank that provides research in the fields of economic policy, foreign policy, government policy, and the social sciences. In 2001 it began America's Response to Terrorism, an online project that provides briefings and analysis to the public. The institution has also published several books on topics of national security and the War on Terror.

Carnegie Endowment for International Peace
1779 Massachusetts Ave. NW, Washington, DC   20036-2103
(202) 483-7600 • fax: (202) 483-1840
e-mail: info@carnegieendowment.org
Web site: www.carnegieendowment.org

The Carnegie Endowment for International Peace, a private, nonpartisan organization, encourages the United States to take an active role in international relations. The institution promotes foreign policy that encourages nations to work together and create global change. *Foreign Policy* magazine is the bimonthly publication of the Carnegie Endowment; other reports and publications can be found on its Web site.

Cato Institute
1000 Massachusetts Ave. NW, Washington, DC   20001-5403
(202) 842-0200 • fax: (202) 842-3490
e-mail: cato@cato.org
Web site: www.cato.org

The Cato Institute is a libertarian organization that bases much of its public policy analysis on Jeffersonian philosophy. The institute promotes the spread of American political values and free-market systems but questions the efficacy of military intervention abroad. The institute publishes the *Cato Journal* three times a year, coinciding with the end of their triannual conferences. Other published materials covering all areas of public policy can be found on the group's Web site.

Center for Defense Information (CDI)
1779 Massachusetts Ave. NW, Suite 615
Washington, DC   20036
(202) 332-0600 • fax: (202) 462-4559
e-mail: info@cdi.org
Web site: www.cdi.org

The CDI is a nonpartisan organization that researches global security. It provides information to policy makers and the general public about security policy, global hot spots, and defense budgeting. It publishes the monthly *Defense Monitor*, which contains many articles and op-ed pieces on national security, homeland defense, and foreign policy.

Center for Security Policy (CSP)
1901 Pennsylvania Ave. NW, Washington, DC   20006
(202) 835-9077 • fax: (202) 835-9066
e-mail: info@centerforsecuritypolicy.org
Web site: www.centerforsecuritypolicy.org

The CSP is a nonprofit organization that informs the debate and ensures effective action on vital national security issues. The CSP believes America should have a strong national defense and should promote security through military, economic, and diplomatic means. The organization's Web site details several CSP projects relating to terrorism, Middle East policy, energy security, and national defense.

Central Intelligence Agency (CIA)
Office of Public Affairs, Washington, DC   20505
(703) 482-0623 • fax: (703) 482-1739
Web site: www.cia.gov

The CIA coordinates national intelligence gathering and analysis that impacts U.S. security. The CIA is an independent agency, responsible to the president and accountable to the American people through the intelligence oversight committees of both houses of the U.S. Congress. The CIA publishes a *Factbook on Intelligence* and other reports that are available on its Web site.

Federal Bureau of Investigation (FBI)
935 Pennsylvania Ave. NW, Washington, DC   20535
(202) 324-3000
Web site: www.fbi.gov

The FBI, the principal investigative arm of the U.S. Department of Justice, is a law enforcement branch that contends with federal crimes, including countering terrorism and foreign intelligence gathering on U.S. soil. The FBI is also often called upon to aid other law enforcement bodies at the federal, state, and local levels. Speeches, press releases, and other issue papers pertaining to FBI activities are available on its Web site.

The Heritage Foundation
214 Massachusetts Ave. NE, Washington, DC   20002-4999
(202) 546-4400 • fax: (202) 546-8328
e-mail: info@heritage.org
Web site: www.heritage.org

The Heritage Foundation, a conservative think tank, provides research and information on current public policies. The foundation has supported the deployment of troops to Iraq and other presidential initiatives concerning the War on Terror. The Heritage Foundation Web site provides numerous online publications analyzing national security and other areas of government policy.

Institute for Policy Studies (IPS)
1112 Sixteenth St. NW, Suite 600, Washington, DC   20036
(202) 234-9382 • fax: (202) 387-7915

Web site: www.ips-dc.org

The IPS is a progressive think tank that promotes a society built around justice and nonviolence. Numerous articles and interviews on September 11 and terrorism are available on its Web site. It also features a series of Iraq reports and sponsors programs on nuclear security, foreign policy, and the Middle East.

The Middle East Policy Council (MEPC)
1730 M St. NW, Suite 512, Washington, DC   20036
(202) 296-6767 • fax: (202) 296-5791
e-mail: info@mepc.org
Web site: www.mepc.org

The MEPC works to inform and induce debate and discussion about U.S. government policies involving the Middle East. The organization publishes the quarterly journal *Middle East Policy* that has covered issues such as the U.S. role in Iraq and the War on Terror. Its Web site offers suggested readings and other publications as well as links to other Web sites concerning the Middle East.

National Security Agency
9800 Savage Rd., Fort Meade, MD   20755-6248
(301) 688-6524 • fax: (301) 688-6198
e-mail: nsapao@nsa.gov
Web site: www.nsa.gov

The NSA is a government organization that is in charge of protecting national security information through encryption and deciphering foreign intelligence. The organization's Web site houses press releases, speeches, Congressional testimony, and other documents about its operation and mission.

Rand Corporation
PO Box 2138, Santa Monica, CA   90407-2138
(310) 393-0411 • fax: (310) 393-4818
Web site: www.rand.org

The Rand Corporation is a nonprofit institution that helps improve policy and decision making through research and analysis. The corporation has studied terrorism for thirty years and has published numerous books on that subject as well as foreign policy and national security. Research papers on these topics are also available on the Rand Web site.

U.S. Department of Homeland Security (DHS)
Washington, DC   20528
(202) 282-8000
Web site: www.dhs.gov

Created just after the September 11, 2001, terrorist attacks, the DHS was envisioned as a central agency that could coordinate federal, state, and local resources to prevent or respond to threats to the American homeland. The DHS contains many subdivisions that deal specifically with trade, immigration, preparedness, and research. The DHS Web site contains speeches and Congressional testimony by DHS representatives, as well as mission statements and department performance records.

Washington Institute for Near East Policy
1828 L St. NW, Suite 1050, Washington, DC   20036
(202) 452-0650 • fax: (202) 223-5364
e-mail: info@washingtoninstitute.org
Web site: www.washingtoninstitute.org

The Washington Institute for Near East Policy is an organization dedicated to providing nonpartisan information to assist lawmakers and politicians in creating effective policies concerning the Middle East. The institute encourages policies in which the United States plays an active role in the region, helping both Americans and Middle Easterners. Many articles on topics pertaining to the region are available on the group's Web site.

Bibliography of Books

Graham Allison *Nuclear Terrorism: The Ultimate Preventable Catastrophe.* New York: Owl, 2005.

Ali M. Ansari *Confronting Iran: The Failure of American Foreign Policy and the Next Great Crisis in the Middle East.* New York: Perseus, 2006.

Stewart A. Baker and John Kavanagh, eds. *Patriot Debates: Experts Debate the USA Patriot Act.* Washington, DC: American Bar Association, 2005.

Peter Brookes *A Devil's Triangle: Terrorism, Weapons of Mass Destruction, and Rogue States.* Lanham, MD: Rowman & Littlefield, 2005.

Richard Butler *Fatal Choice: Nuclear Weapons and the Illusion of Missile Defense.* Boulder, CO: Westview, 2001.

Kurt Campbell and Michael O'Hanlon *Hard Power: The New Politics of National Security.* New York: Basic, 2006.

Victor D. Cha and David C. Kang *Nuclear North Korea: A Debate on Engagement Strategies.* New York: Columbia University Press, 2005.

Nancy Chang *Silencing Political Dissent: How Post–September 11 Anti-terrorism Measures Threaten Our Civil Liberties.* New York: Seven Stories, 2002.

Council on Foreign Relations	*National Security Consequences of U.S. Oil Dependency.* Independent Task Force Report No. 58. Washington, DC: Council on Foreign Relations, 2007.
M. Katherine B. Darmer, Robert M. Baird, and Stuart E. Rosenbaum, eds.	*Civil Liberties vs. National Security in a Post 9/11 World.* Amherst, NY: Prometheus, 2004.
Alan M. Dershowitz	*Why Terrorism Works: Understanding the Threat, Responding to the Challenge.* New Haven, CT: Yale University Press, 2003.
Amitai Etzioni	*How Patriotic Is the Patriot Act? Freedom Versus Security in the Age of Terrorism.* New York: Routledge, 2004.
David Frum and Richard Perle	*An End to Evil: How to Win the War on Terror.* New York: Random House, 2003.
Thomas Graham Jr.	*Common Sense on Weapons of Mass Destruction.* Seattle: University of Washington Press, 2004.
Nadine Gurr and Benjamin Cole	*The New Face of Terrorism: Threats from Weapons of Mass Destruction.* London: I.B. Tauris, 2002.
Stephen Hess and Marvin L. Kalb, eds.	*The Media and the War on Terrorism.* Washington, DC: Brookings Institution, 2003.

Mark Hitchcock   *Iran: The Coming Crisis: Radical Islam, Oil, and the Nuclear Threat.* Sis-
ters, OR: Multnomah, 2006.

Russell Howard,   *Homeland Security and Terrorism:
James Forest, and   Readings and Interpretations.* New
Joanne Moore,   York: McGraw-Hill, 2006.
eds.

Peter R. Lavoy,   *Planning the Unthinkable: How New
Scott D. Sagan,   Powers Will Use Nuclear, Biological,
and James J.   and Chemical Weapons.* Ithaca, NY:
Wirtz, eds.   Cornell University Press, 2000.

Richard C. Leone   *The War on Our Freedoms: Civil Lib-
and Greg Anrig   erties in an Age of Terrorism.* New
Jr., eds.   York: PublicAffairs, 2003.

Gavan   *Target North Korea: Pushing North
McCormack   Korea to the Brink of Nuclear Catastrophe.* New York: Nation, 2004.

Philip M.   *Secrecy Wars: National Security, Pri-
Melanson   vacy, and the Public's Right to Know.*
Washington, DC: Brassey's, 2001.

John Mueller   *Overblown: How Politicians and the
Terrorism Industry Inflate National
Security Threats, and Why We Believe
Them.* New York: Free Press, 2006.

Karl P. Mueller et   *Striking First: Preemptive and Preven-
al.   tive Attack in U.S. National Security
Policy.* Santa Monica, CA: Rand,
2007.

Thomas E. Ricks   *Fiasco: The American Military Adventure in Iraq.* New York: Penguin,
2006.

Sergey N.
Rumyantsev

Biological Weapon: A Terrible Reality? Profound Delusion? Skillful Swindling? New York: Vantage, 2006.

Gary Schmitt

Of Men and Materiel: The Crisis in Defense Spending. Washington, DC: AEI, 2007.

Donald Snow

National Security for a New Era: Globalization and Geopolitics. New York: Longman, 2006.

Robert Spencer

Onward Muslim Soldiers: How Jihad Still Threatens America and the West. Washington, DC: Regnery, 2003.

Index